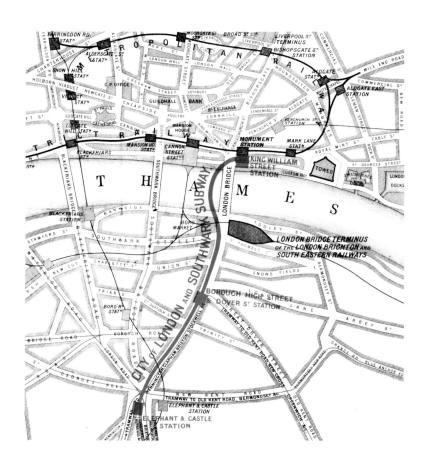

THE BIRTH
OF THE TUBES

Capital Transport

Picture credits

Illustrations are from the Capital Transport collection except the following, the copyright in which is held by those named:

London Transport Museum, TfL: Front cover lower, 1, 9, 10 centre, 13, 16 upper, 18 upper, 19 lower, 25, 28, 38, 49, 52, 54 upper, 64, 65 lower, 68, 69, 74, 75, 77, 80, 81, 83, 84, 89 lower, 90, 92, 94.

Alamy: 5.

Antony Badsey-Ellis collection: 12, 39 top, 87.

Piers Connor: 56, 57.

Hulton Getty: 21 lower, 42.

Doug Rose: 61.

Royal Borough of Kensington and Chelsea: 47.

Colourisations: The photos and postcards on pages 8, 55, 59, 60, 63, 75 lower, 79 and 84 lower are either historical hand coloured postcards or modern colourisations. In the case of the latter, all care has been taken to render the colours as accurately as possible from information available. Postcards from the time may also include some artistic licence. None of these images should be regarded as definitive sources for particular colours, though all give a good general impression.

ISBN 978-1-85414-441-6

Published by
Capital Transport Publishing
www.capitaltransport.com

Printed by Parksons Graphics

Contents

Author's Note

Many books have been written about London's tube railways. In this book, I take a different angle, and see how they were viewed by the press of the day, through the use of newspaper and magazine reports, as well as through the publicity and marketing materials that were created by the companies themselves.

In the period from 1890 to 1914, a large number of newspapers were published – in the days before the internet, television, and even radio, this was the way that people found out what was going on. Journalists were keen to inform their readers about the latest advances, and the companies were keen to publicize their new services by arranging for visits to construction sites and supplying text to form the basis of articles.

I could not have written this book without the help of Jim Whiting, who has spent many hours locating interesting articles and illustrations in the archives of London. The London Transport Museum collection has supplied a number of the pictures, thanks to their on-line catalogue. Mike Horne, Paul Hadley, Douglas Rose, David Burton, and Brian Hardy have all provided helpful comments after reviewing drafts. Piers Connor provided considerable help with the carriage drawings on pages 56 and 57. As ever, I am grateful to my wife, Wendy, for putting up with the many hours of research and writing that have gone into this book.

Amersham, July 2019

Front cover upper The Baker Street station of the Baker Street & Waterloo Railway shortly before its opening in March 1906, showing the shared style of the many stations opened in 1906 and 1907.

Front cover lower Interior of a carriage of the Central London Railway, in a drawing produced c.1901. With the sliding doors at the carriage end open there is a good view across the end gates into the next carriage. Note also the early provision of 'straphangers', an import from America where use is recorded as early as 1893.

Facing page The first demonstration of an electric locomotive occurred at the Berlin Trade Fair of 1879, where Dr Werner von Siemens exhibited a short railway. Two years later, the first electrically operated tube railway was proposed for central London.

A Small Beginning

Two developments within a short time of each other paved the way for London's deep level tubes. The first was the invention of a tunnelling shield which enabled a tubular excavation of clay at a deep level and provided a chamber in which men could put in place cast iron linings to form a permanent tunnel. The second was the invention of the electric motor, first demonstrated at an exhibition in 1879 by German engineer Dr Werner von Siemens.

When the first parliamentary bill for an electric tube railway was presented in 1881, the first underground railway, the Metropolitan, had been in operation for eighteen years. This, and the Metropolitan District Railway which followed it, had to use steam locomotives and were built using a highly disruptive method whereby a large trench was dug, usually in the road and then covered over to provide a tunnel along which the railway would run.

The tube railway proposed in 1881 was to run two-thirds of a mile between Trafalgar Square and Waterloo, and a subsequent extension was envisaged to the Royal Exchange via Stamford Street, Bankside and back across the Thames near Southwark Bridge. A 60ft stretch of the planned line was built using the cut-and-cover method (as used for much of the Metropolitan Railway) below Northumberland Avenue before the company, The Charing Cross and Waterloo Electric Railway Company, was dissolved in 1886.

The First Tube

The public were admitted to the first tube railway in London, Britain, and the world, on 18 December 1890. Over the past 27 years they had become accustomed to travelling beneath London's streets on the Metropolitan and Metropolitan District Railways, but these both used familiar steam locomotives hauling a series of carriages in which passengers were segregated by class of ticket. The City & South London Railway (C&SLR), the first tube railway, was rather different. Small electric locomotives pulled almost windowless carriages through the tunnels. Passengers boarded from platforms at the end of the carriages, and inside they were seated on long cloth-covered seats placing them sideways to the direction of travel, with only one class of ticket provided. It was originally promoted as the City of London and Southwark Subway. According to Printz Holman, probably the leading authority on this line, the word subway was used to disguise the fact from parliament and the Board of Trade that this was in fact a railway that was planned rather than a pedestrian walkway.

The C&SLR was the second tunnel cored beneath the bed of the Thames using Greathead's shield. The first had been the Tower Subway, opened in 1870, near to the Tower of London. Although not a financial success, it had demonstrated that the shield was a workable technology. Greathead went on to help promote and build the C&SLR, which was to be a cable-hauled tube railway

This line drawing shows the conditions at the tunnel face as the C&SLR tunnels were being driven, although there is a degree of artistic licence. The size of the tunnel has also been exaggerated, as in reality they were only 10 ft 2 ins diameter, and so the workmen should be over half the height of the tunnel. Seven men are shown: three in the background, excavating the face with picks, one in the middle-ground, probably shovelling the spoil into the tub on the trolley, and three in the foreground. Of the latter, the one on the right is injecting grout from the tank through holes in the tunnel segment to fill the space between the clay and the cast iron tunnel, the centre man is steadying the spoil tub, and the man on the left is holding a pair of shovels. The scene is illuminated by nine candles.

between King William Street in the City of London, and the Elephant & Castle. Construction started in 1886 from a shaft sunk in the Thames, with the running tunnels being mined out both northwards and southwards. Once the riskiest part of the work was complete – this being the under-river tunnels – more shafts were sunk at the sites for each station along the line, and more miners began to carve the tunnels through the London clay.

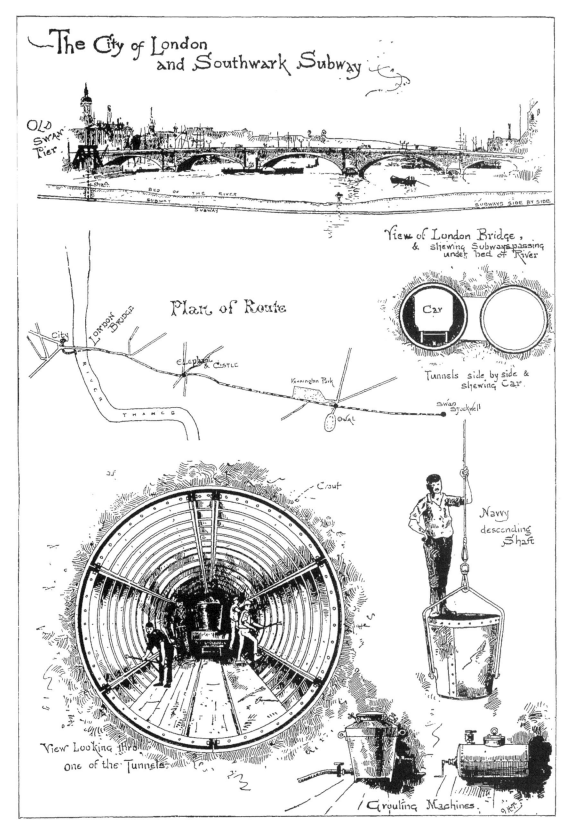

The City of London and Southwark Subway

OLD SWAN PIER

Shaft

BED OF THE RIVER

SUBWAY   SUBWAY

SUBWAYS SIDE BY SIDE

View of London Bridge,
& shewing Subways passing
under bed of River

Plan of Route

LONDON BRIDGE

City

RIVER THAMES

Elephant & Castle

Kennington Park

Oval

Swan Stockwell

Car

Tunnels side by side &
shewing Car.

Grout

Navvy
descending
Shaft

View Looking thro'
one of the Tunnels.

Grouting Machines.

This collection of drawings published in the *Penny Illustrated Paper* to illustrate an accompanying article shows a map of the route together with a cross-section of the under-river tunnels. The grouting machines are shown as being of particular interest, and the view into the tunnel again exaggerates the tunnel size, but better shows the temporary tracks installed to move the spoil tubs on small trolleys. The drawing of the navvy descending the shaft demonstrates the less rigorous attitude to health and safety than is present at tunnelling sites today.

THE CITY AND SOUTHWARK SUBWAY

The Greathead shield was a metal cylinder just under 6 feet long and about 11 feet in diameter. It was open at each end, but had a central partition that gave it rigidity, and which had a rectangular opening. Behind the partition, a set of hydraulic rams were located. The tunnel was bored by miners excavating the clay in front of the shield through the opening in the partition. Once about 20 inches of clay had been cut away, hand pumps were used to extend the hydraulic rams, pressing the whole shield forwards. Steel cutters on the front edge trimmed the roughly cut clay, whilst behind the rams, but still within the protection of the metal cylinder, seven heavy cast iron pieces were manhandled into position and bolted together to form a ring of completed tunnel.

FROM King William Street to the Elephant and Castle in 3 minutes and 40 seconds. This was done last Wednesday by a party of gentlemen invited by the directors of the City and Southwark Subway Company to take part in an experimental run on their partly completed line. Two carriages, each capable of containing thirty-four passengers, started from the City terminus, and before the occupants had fairly settled themselves in their places, pulled up at their destination, having traversed the intervening space of nearly a mile and a half at a high rate of speed. The trip was made in perfect comfort in a pure atmosphere, and afforded a pleasing contrast to the various means of locomotion in the metropolis, both above and below ground. The possibilities of this novel line were fairly demonstrated, and none could resist the conviction that it is the pioneer of a new system which is destined to prove of immense service to the dwellers in the metropolis.

Stations on the C&SLR, except for the City terminus, followed a similar style with domed roof housing.

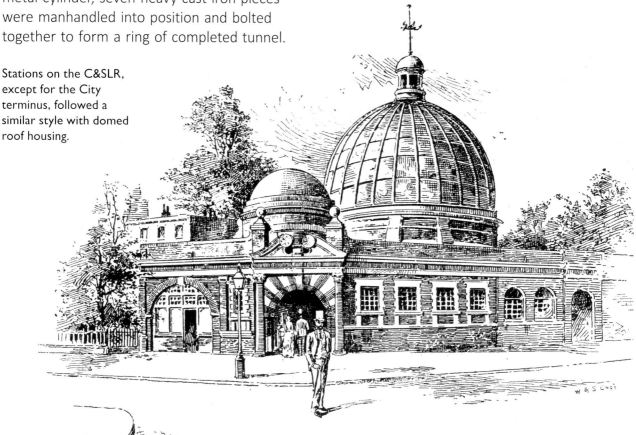

By 1890, the original plans for the railway had changed considerably. At its southern end, it had been extended from Elephant & Castle to Stockwell. The idea of cable haulage had been dropped, and the company made a brave decision, at what was a very late stage, to try the new force of electricity to move their trains. In 1889, contracts were signed with the Salford-based firm of Mather and Platt to provide all of the necessary electrical equipment for the railway. A power station was built at the Stockwell depot and fourteen locomotives were provided.

Above ground, new stations were built at five sites south of the Thames, as single-storey brick buildings with stone detailing, and surmounted by large domes. Passengers paid for their journeys and were admitted via turnstiles, without the need for a ticket, for a flat fare was charged regardless of distance travelled. Large hydraulic lifts took them down to white-tiled passageways leading to the platforms.

Top A rare photograph of a C&SLR train at an unidentified station (being a single platform, and taken before the line was extended in 1900, it was one of the stations between Borough and Oval). Train 13 is hauled by one of the original 1890 locomotives, and comprises three carriages of 1893-4 vintage, which had slightly larger windows than the original 'padded cells'.

Above Inside one of the original carriages of the City & South London Railway showing the small windows and high upholstery that gave rise to the nickname for these carriages.

Below The C&SLR was formally opened by the Prince of Wales over a month before the public service began. He was received by the company officials at King William Street station, then travelled by train to Stockwell. This is the cover of the menu produced for the banquet that was held in Stockwell depot upon the Prince's arrival.

Bottom The turnstiles, or 'pay gates', at stations on the C&SLR. On payment of the flat fare, the booking office clerk would release the gate for the passenger to pass through.

SOUTH LONDON is in the proud position of being the possessor of the first electric railway in the metropolis. The ceremony on Tuesday was very properly associated with the Prince of Wales, because the affair is really of national importance. If the City and South London Railway succeeds, as every one hopes it will, a most difficult problem will have been solved. You cannot put more in a bottle than it will hold, and our streets are already choked with cabs, omnibuses and tramway-cars, that it is not easy to see how any more travelling facilities on the surface of the ground can be provided.

What remains now to see is how the railway will work practically, and the public will be able to test this for itself in about a fortnight's time. At present the arrangements are such as will delight the great body of middle-class travellers, who have shortened their tempers and their lives by the annoyances which ordinary railways subject them to. There will be no more imperious demands to show your tickets; no more insolences from booking-office clerks; no more queues at ticket windows, waiting impatiently while some old lady is making tremulous inquiries how to get to Timbuctoo or some other out-of-the-way place, and asking how much it will cost to get there. There is but one class; it is "two-pence all the way, or any distance;" and the only thing you have to do is pass through a turnstile and put your money down. There is a delightful simplicity about this arrangement which appeals to everyone.

As to the abolition of class distinction, which seems to have frightened some, is there anything new in this? Is not the omnibus run on the same plan? I can see nothing to object to in the electric railway having only one class.

Below This announcement appeared in a number of publications following the opening of the new line to the public on 18 December 1890, suggesting that the wording was supplied by the C&SLR. That first day of public opening is reported to have been during a spell of exceptionally bad weather with heavy snowfalls, from which the new underground railway was immune.

Being a pioneer has always been risky, and the C&SLR proved this in 1890. The line was officially opened on 4 November by the Prince of Wales with a large ceremony. However, it was over a month before the public were allowed to use the line, because the company was finding that its power station was insufficient for the task of running a full service. Changes were made, including refitting the lamps in the signals and on the platforms to use gas. Nothing could be done about the carriage lighting though, and passengers became used to the lamps dimming to a dull red glow as the trains valiantly climbed the steep gradient into the King William Street terminus.

Changes were made in the early years. Tickets appeared in 1892; this allowed return tickets to be sold, reducing queues at ticket offices. The almost windowless carriages were not popular (being referred to as 'padded cells'), and within a year new carriages had been ordered with larger windows (although these augmented, rather than replaced the originals).

THE NEW ELECTRIC RAILWAY

On Thursday traffic was commenced over the new underground electric railway between the City and Stockwell. Considerable public interest was shown in the new route, but a five minutes' service of trains kept the platforms clear. The intermediate stations on the line between King William Street and the Swan, Stockwell, are: The Borough, Elephant and Castle, Kennington, and the Oval – the through journey occupying a little over 20 minutes.

A later illustration showing, at Euston station, one of the original locomotives hauling the second design of carriage, fitted with deeper windows.

The Waterloo & City Railway

The opening of the C&SLR resulted in a number of tube railway schemes being deposited with Parliament in 1891 for approval. Parliamentary delays prevented any from being given Royal Assent until 1893, and of these only one was opened by the end of the decade. This was the Waterloo & City Railway, and it achieved this because it was financially backed by the London & South Western Railway, a main-line company that had its terminus at Waterloo. The W&CR was designed to speed its passengers onwards to their jobs in the City of London, and saving them from catching a bus or hiring a cab.

Learning from the C&SLR, the new line was built with larger tunnels that would accommodate larger carriages. Rather than use locomotives, the four-carriage trains had motors fitted onto their end carriages, which also had drivers' cabs. Like its predecessor, the W&CR used turnstiles in place of tickets at first, as there was only one class of travel, and they too began to introduce tickets about a year after opening.

At Waterloo the station was placed within the arches that support the main-line station, with stairs and ramps for access. At the City station (only renamed Bank in 1940), the platforms were in large tube tunnels. A long, sloping tunnel was the only way in and out, and for many years this tired the legs of exiting passengers. These were (and remain) the only stations on the line, and between them a pair of tunnels was constructed using Greathead shields, passing beneath the Thames just upstream of Blackfriars Bridge.

The new tube railway opened on 8 August 1898. Four trains provided the entire peak service, and within a year it was transporting over 10,000 passengers every weekday.

This drawing by Henri Lanos was published in *The Graphic*, and shows a workman emerging from an airlock constructed in one of the tunnels on the W&CR. The airlocks were installed where the tunnels passed beneath the District Railway on the north bank of the Thames at Blackfriars, to reduce the risk of subsidence by allowing the tunnels to be built under compressed air. The ghostly effect is due to water vapour condensing from the air; above the airlock a pressure gauge can be seen. Until the science behind working in compressed air was better understood, workers risked injury or even death from "the bends", a condition in which bubbles of dissolved nitrogen formed in the blood as they moved from the compressed air to normal pressure.

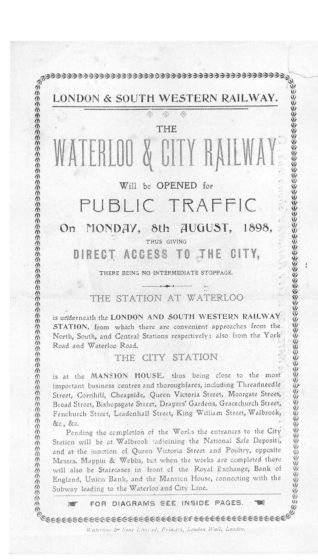

LONDON & SOUTH WESTERN RAILWAY.

THE

WATERLOO & CITY RAILWAY

Will be OPENED for

PUBLIC TRAFFIC

On MONDAY, 8th AUGUST, 1898,

THUS GIVING

DIRECT ACCESS TO THE CITY,

THERE BEING NO INTERMEDIATE STOPPAGE.

THE STATION AT WATERLOO

is underneath the LONDON AND SOUTH WESTERN RAILWAY STATION, from which there are convenient approaches from the North, South, and Central Stations respectively; also from the York Road and Waterloo Road.

THE CITY STATION

is at the MANSION HOUSE, thus being close to the most important business centres and thoroughfares, including Threadneedle Street, Cornhill, Cheapside, Queen Victoria Street, Moorgate Street, Broad Street, Bishopsgate Street, Drapers' Gardens, Gracechurch Street, Fenchurch Street, Leadenhall Street, King William Street, Walbrook, &c., &c.

Pending the completion of the Works the entrances to the City Station will be at Walbrook (adjoining the National Safe Deposit), and at the junction of Queen Victoria Street and Poultry, opposite Messrs. Mappin & Webbs, but when the works are completed there will also be Staircases in front of the Royal Exchange, Bank of England, Union Bank, and the Mansion House, connecting with the Subway leading to the Waterloo and City Line.

☞ FOR DIAGRAMS SEE INSIDE PAGES. ☜

Waterlow & Sons Limited, Printers, London Wall, London.

Above Details of the construction of the new tube railways were eagerly followed by the press, and especially the technical publications. This plan and section, published in *The Engineer*, shows the route of the W&CR tunnels beneath the Thames. The shaft from where the tunnels were started was sunk in the river from a pier. The deep bed of 'fine sand and ballast' beneath the District Railway (on the right-hand side of the section) was the primary cause of this section being built under compressed air.

Below left Press report from the *Daily Telegraph* dated 9 August 1898.

Below Exterior and interior views of the first design of train on the Waterloo & City Railway. Each carriage had a single hand-operated sliding door for passengers to enter and exit. This area separated the carriages into two compartments, each with interior sliding doors – quite a luxury for so short a journey.

NEW RAILWAY UNDER
THE THAMES

Yesterday morning, at eight o'clock, the first train-load of passengers left Waterloo, on the Waterloo and City railway, for the Mansion House, accomplishing the underground journey, a distance of a mile and a half, in a little over five minutes. There were about 100 people in the cars, and the subsequent services conveyed the full complement of passengers – 208 - from the South-Western terminus to the new station in the City. Throughout the morning, and in fact during the whole day, there was not the slightest hitch in the working of the electric railway.

Yesterday, of course, nearly everyone bought tickets or paid the single fare at the turnstiles; consequently there was, up to 10.30, a continuously dense crowd of people at the booking office. This will be avoided in future. The South-Western Railway have arranged that passengers can book right through to the City from the suburban stations, and season ticket-holders can have their ordinary season tickets stamped with the pass of the new railway.

The Central London Railway

The most obvious route in central London for an underground railway was the east-west alignment marked out by the Bayswater Road, Oxford Street, Holborn, and Cheapside. This line bisected the Inner Circle railway created in 1884 when the Metropolitan and Metropolitan District Railways finally joined their routes together, and passed through the affluent west end, the main shopping district, and the City of London. It was therefore not surprising when the Central London Railway was promoted along this route in 1891.

A mining syndicate put up some of the money for the railway and, after a public share offering raised further capital, construction work began in early 1896. A pair of tunnels was constructed between the Bank junction in the City of London and Shepherd's Bush in the west. With three exceptions, the white-tiled platforms were at the same level, in between the tracks, with stairs leading up to lift landings and lifts then taking passengers up to street level. At Notting Hill Gate, Chancery Lane, and Post Office (now St Paul's), the platforms were at different levels, and overlapping, to keep them beneath the narrower streets above. At most of the stations the platforms were aligned at a higher level than the tracks between stations, as this helped the trains to slow as they approached, and accelerate away downhill from the platforms.

The station buildings were clad in part-baked terracotta, giving them a pale pink-brown colour, and were designed to accommodate future storeys being built above – this would provide further income for the railway. Bank was not provided with a building, the ticket hall being constructed beneath the road junction and surrounded by a circular pedestrian subway that would provide a safe route to cross the junction for all, not just railway passengers. Five lifts descended in separate shafts to a concourse between the platforms. Beyond Bank a pair of sidings indicated the direction that the railway intended to extend, towards Liverpool Street. In order to avoid tunnelling beneath the vaults of the Bank of England, this left the platforms on a very sharp curve.

The line was opened by the Prince of Wales on Wednesday 27 June 1900, with the usual specially invited guests in attendance (including Mark Twain on this occasion). A large celebratory banquet was held in the Wood Lane depot for the line, beyond Shepherd's Bush station. Following this the railway opened to the public on Tuesday 31 July 1900, the five weeks between the two dates presumably allowing the contractors to complete the last details for the railway.

Fares on the line were a flat 2d at first, leading the railway to quickly acquire the nickname of the Twopenny Tube. This was also picked up by the 1900 revival of the Gilbert and Sullivan comic opera Patience, featuring the "very delectable, highly respectable, Twopenny Tube young man".

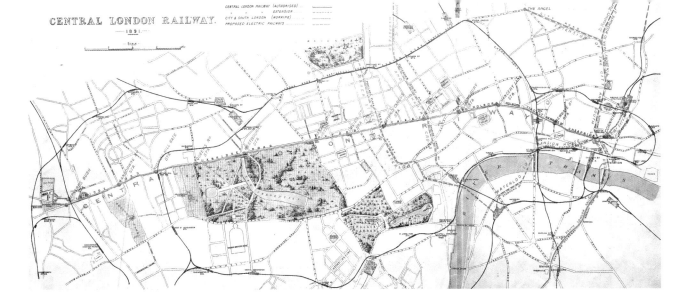

THE TWOPENNY TUBE

The Central London Railway is finished at last, and the people who like to live in Shepherd's Bush, whoever they may be, will be able to arrive at the Bank after a subterranean journey of twenty-five minutes, including stopping.

The Twopenny Tube should be a very popular railway. As a means of transport it is rapid, it is smooth, it is well-lighted. The carriages, for twopence, are too luxurious. Whoever rides for that modest sum, and sits on a well-padded seat, automatically correct in form so that it supports his back, will grumble ever after at the ordinary first-class carriage seat, which does nothing of the kind. It thrusts a lump of stuffing into his shoulders, and leaves him doubled up, with his chin on his chest.

It is not certain that the uniform charge of twopence will be maintained. For the whole journey it is ludicrously cheap; from one station to the next it is rather dear. It seems to be decided that there will be only one class. No doubt there would never be enough time to sort out the passengers.

Extracts from The Londoner magazine, 30 June 1900 with the first reference to the CLR's nickname

A TWENTY MINUTES' RUN.

FROM THE BANK TO SHEPHERD'S BUSH.

There never was a quieter opening of a railway than that in which the Prince of Wales yesterday took part after travelling from the Bank to Shepherd's Bush on the new Central London Railway. It may have been native modesty on the part of the directors of the line; it may have been that in the proceedings they wished to typify the noiselessness and speed of electric traction; it may have been that they agreed with the harassed Cabinet Minister who asked why such undertakings could not be opened at night by a policeman. But from whatever causes, this much is certain—that the ceremony was the simplest and the speeches were the briefest on record. There was, in fact, only one speech, which was delivered by the Prince of Wales in the intervals of the refreshment with which the company brightened the proceedings. The Prince said, " I have great pleasure in declaring the Central London Railway open. I am sure it will prove a great boon to our great City; and I think Sir Benjamin Baker, its engineer, is to be congratulated on the success with which he has carried out the undertaking. I ask you to drink with me success to the Central London Railway." Which the company did with great enthusiasm. And that was all, positively all, though among the company who had preceded or who had accompanied the Prince of Wales to Shepherd's Bush depot, where the opening took place, there were many who could, and possibly who would, have contributed instruction and information had they been called upon. Sir Henry Oakley was there as the chairman of the company, Lord Rothschild, Lord Colville of Culross, Mr. Labouchere, with whose views on speech-making the proceedings were no doubt thoroughly in accord, Sir Francis Knollys (a director), the Lord Mayor (in private dress), Sir Alexander Binnie, Sir Benjamin Baker, Sir W. Preece; and such an array of railway managers, engineers, and railway directors, that had an accident occurred to the electric train one would imagine that the whole traffic of London and the provinces would have been dislocated. No such accident occurred, however. The electric train, with its seven carriages, glided with an ease that was almost magical out of the brilliantly-lit Bank Station into the great tube that has been cut into the London clay for over six miles westwards, slipped through brightly-lighted white-tiled stations one after the other, until, twenty minutes after it had started, it climbed smoothly up into sunlight once more at Shepherd's Bush. The train did not stop at the passengers' station, but at the depot, half a mile further on; and here, before the Prince's speech, a company numbering some five hundred people spent an instructive half-hour in examining the great purring dynamos, and in asking the engineers questions about the capacity of the boilers. As there was no one to give information of any kind whatever, so it is impossible to say when the new railway will be open to the public; but next week was a rumoured date, and the running of the trains yesterday was at any rate perfect. The lifts are, however, not yet all in order.

A press cutting from the day after the royal opening of the line in June 1900. Its reference to the train climbing into sunlight at Shepherd's Bush is a bit misleading and refers to the end of the line at Wood Lane.

The trains followed the practice of the C&SLR in having carriages hauled by electric locomotives. The latter were large 'camel-back' machines which soon gained notoriety along the line for the vibration that they induced in the buildings above. A committee was appointed by the Board of Trade in 1901, which placed the blame on the weight and design of the locomotives, and the construction of the track. The company was quick to respond, and ordered new motor carriages which replaced the locomotives in 1903. This was an expensive problem, as the locomotives were mostly scrapped.

Other complaints arose about the atmosphere in the tunnels, with letters to the press soon after opening. Rumours spread that the air was poisonous, disease-ridden, or contained too much carbon dioxide, and in late 1901 another committee was appointed to investigate. Its research showed that, aside from the slightly earthy smell, there was

nothing at all the matter with the air. The CLR was relieved at this result, but decided nonetheless to install an enormous fan at the Shepherd's Bush end of the line. Each night, after the trains had stopped running, the doors at all intermediate stations were closed and the fan was used to suck air through the tunnels from Bank. It was not particularly effective, and the company installed further fans at some stations in an attempt to improve matters.

Above A view of the platform at Notting Hill Gate at the time of opening. The platforms on the Central London Railway were of wooden planks, though these were replaced by stone slabs following a serious fire on the Paris Metro in 1903.

Top left Gatemen at their posts show how labour intensive the early tubes were. Two of the cars are labelled for 'Smoking'.

Left Passengers board the first train to leave Shepherd's Bush station on the Central London Railway in a photograph that appeared in the *Black and White Budget* magazine.

The opening for traffic of the Central London Railway ought to be the signal for further electric underground travel in London. As it happened the opening day was a breezy one, after a period of stifling heat. Even the inside of an omnibus was tolerable and the underground railways of the older pattern were endurable. Hence the first contest between the new style of locomotion and the old was practically confined to the points of speed, cheapness and general convenience. Novelty, of course, entered to some extent into consideration. Omnibus drivers, missing familiar faces on their morning journey Cityward, comforted themselves with the reflection that regular customers had been temporarily attracted by the new route, and certainly there were not a few passengers whose trips were of an experimental character. However, the coolness, the cleanliness, the rapidity, and the cheapness of travel – 2d for eight miles – are bound to have appealed to those who took experimental trips, to say nothing of those whom the railway will benefit physically and financially.

The omnibus fare from Shepherd's Bush to the Bank is 5d, or 10d for the return journey. The workingman obviously will not pay 10d when he can travel the same distance more quickly for 2d.

The line has already been nicknamed the 'Refrigerator' on account of the cool, breezy atmosphere.

From *Black and White Budget* magazine, 11 August 1900

As well as the Gilbert & Sullivan reference to the Twopenny Tube, a song of (almost) the same name was written in 1900. The music and lyrics were published, and the cover is shown here, featuring some small drawings of a platform, station, and carriage interior. R.G. Knowles was a popular music-hall entertainer who was brought up in America, and came to England in 1891.

All of the stations on the CLR were provided with single-storey buildings with terracotta cladding, with the exception of Bank which was entirely below street level. The windows with their gently arched top let light into the ticket halls, from where lifts descended to the lower levels. The architect was Harry B. Measures.

This lovely period view of a quiet Holland Park Avenue shows the CLR station being served by a horse bus and an elderly well-to-do lady resting in the foreground with someone who appears to be an attendant of some kind.

One of the original 'camel-back' locomotives that created excessive vibrations in properties along the route, seen here with its crew almost certainly at Wood Lane depot.

Although the C&SLR was the first tube railway in London to provide a single class of carriage, it served a short route from the City. The CLR, shown in this illustration, was the first route to cut across London and provide a means of transport to all classes of people without distinction.

British Museum station is typical of all of the CLR stations in the early days, with a wooden platform and white-tiled walls. This view, from 1903, shows one of the newspaper stalls that were provided for the benefit of customers (as well as the railway company). This station closed in 1933, its platforms being replaced by a new pair to the east providing interchange with the Piccadilly Tube at Holborn station.

Facing page An advertisement for a 'Lightning Parcels Delivery' service introduced by the Central London Railway in 1911.

A Bigger Tube

The Great Northern & City Railway (GN&CR) was the second of the tube railways considered by Parliament in 1892 to be opened. It was a rather unusual line, due to its history. As the name suggests, it was initially supported by the main-line Great Northern Railway (GNR) company, as a way of getting its trains into the City of London. They already ran via what was known as the 'City Widened Lines', a pair of tracks constructed by the Metropolitan Railway between the GNR terminus at King's Cross, and Moorgate Street station. The problem was that this route was busy, as were the GNR tracks between King's Cross and Finsbury Park. A direct route from the latter station to the City would provide a solution.

A problem arose, in that main-line rolling stock would not be able to pass through a tube railway of normal size, and the GNR did not want its passengers to change trains. Greathead, who was the engineer, instead proposed making the tunnels with a diameter of 16 ft. This would allow the GNR to merely uncouple their steam locomotives at Finsbury Park, and a GN&CR electric locomotive would haul the carriages south to the Moorgate terminus.

Unfortunately for the directors of the GN&CR, at around the time that they started construction, in 1898, a new tube railway was promoted to link Wood Green, Finsbury Park, King's Cross, and the Strand. Some of the GNR directors switched their support to the newcomer, and this eventually caused the main line company to withdraw its support altogether. Instead of its main-line carriages running directly into the GN&CR tunnels at Finsbury Park, they insisted on constructing a terminus station in tunnel below their main-line station, thus bottling up the tube railway and forcing passengers into an awkward interchange.

Undeterred, the GN&CR directors pushed ahead, but raising the finance proved difficult without the support of the GNR. Eventually the tunnelling contractors accepted shared in the company as part-payment for their work. The tunnels were still built to accommodate main-line trains, perhaps in the hope that one day the GNR would change their minds. A rather unusual process was used for lining the tunnels, in that the lower half of the cast-iron lining was dismantled soon after their construction, and replaced with brickwork. This was claimed to reduce the cost of the lining, as well as absorb noise in the tunnels.

The railway opened on 14 February 1904, and was never a great success. The need to interchange at Finsbury Park, combined with the short length, meant that it never handled large numbers of passengers.

The GN&CR used an elaborate printing design on their tickets, as shown by this early example.

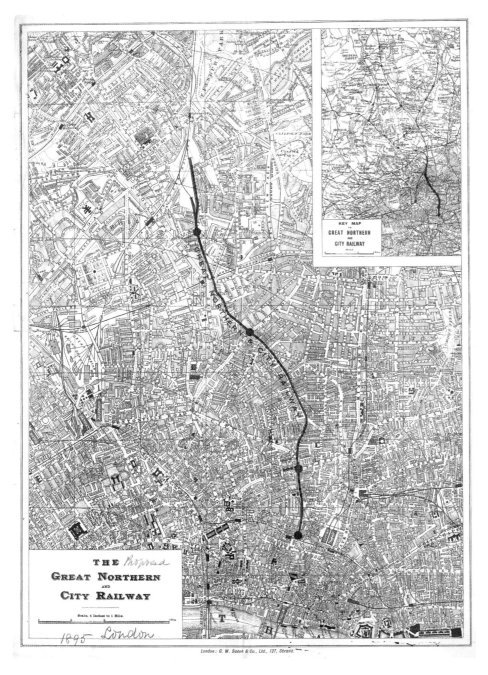

THE *Proposed*
GREAT NORTHERN
AND
CITY RAILWAY

Scale, 6 Inches to 1 Mile.

1895 *London*

London: G. W. Bacon & Co., Ltd., 127, Strand.

KEY MAP
TO
GREAT NORTHERN
AND
CITY RAILWAY

For years past Finsbury Park has been the Clapham Junction of the north – only worse. Business men have given up grumbling at the overcrowding, confusion and delay that turns Finsbury Park every morning and evening into pendemonium. It is not their fault, nor the fault of the Great Northern Railway. Whose physical resources for coping with the sweeping tide of City traffic have long been overtaxed. It is the old, old cry that is heard all over the Metropolis – the cry of the ever-increasing population.

Our latest tube starts at Finsbury Park station, underneath the Great Northern main line, and makes for the heart of the City in an almost straight line. Tapping four distinct districts, Drayton Park, Highbury, Essex-road and Old-street, it reaches Moorgate after three-and-a-half miles of tunnelling. It is the shortest and most rapid rapid route for those who live in these populous districts, and covering the distance in less than half the time previously occupied, and at a third saving in cost, the new line should attain much popularity. The present City terminus is at Moorgate, opposite to and connected with the City and South London station, and at this point there is a very convenient means of interchange.

The Company have fixed upon the Bank as their ultimate terminus, and they are forging ahead with the extension as fast as possible.

Hackney & Kingsland Gazette, Wednesday 17 February 1904

The railway companies had to create maps of their routes as part of their submission to Parliament, when they sought the legal powers to build their new lines. This map is from 1895, when the company asked to extend the time permitted for construction, as (like other tube railways) struggling to raise the necessary finance. Of note is the absence of a station at Highbury, which seems strange given the potential for interchange with the North London Railway. At the north end, the line would join the tracks of the Great Northern Railway and share the surface station at Finsbury Park; this pre-dates the falling-out between the two companies.

The GN&CR had aims to extend to the Bank of England, with a planned terminus on the north side of the bank in Lothbury. Station plans were drawn up, which included what would have been the first use of escalators on a tube railway.

Old Street station was operated jointly by the C&SLR and the GN&CR on the latter's opening in 1904. Both railways were keen to flaunt their electrified status in the early 1900s to differentiate themselves from the steam-operated Metropolitan and District Railways.

Essex Road station has always been one of London's quieter tube stations.

A view of one of the GN&CR stations shortly after opening, with a full complement of staff on show. The larger size of the trains and tunnels is clear to see. The illumination on the platform, provided by the suspended globe lanterns, would normally have been rather lower, but the photographer's flash has lit all the way towards the back of the train. The man on the left with the bowler hat is probably a more senior member of staff.

A LONDON TUBE STATION (GT. NORTHERN & CITY RLY).

Another postcard, this one showing the side of a train in the platform at Finsbury Park in 1904. It makes it obvious that the train is much larger than on other tube railways. The tiled walls of the platform appear very plain and austere compared to the coloured tiles used on subsequent tube railways in London.

A drive to boost traffic on the under-used GN&CR in 1905 saw this advertising postcard being issued. It highlights as many positive features as it can: a high-frequency service; large, well-ventilated trains; and many places of interest near to each of its stations.

Charles Yerkes

The man who enabled more of London's tube railways to be built than any other was an American financier who had been convicted, and then pardoned, for "technical embezzlement" with a reputation for employing somewhat dubious business practices. The impressively moustached Charles Tyson Yerkes (the name rhymes with "turkeys") had already been responsible for the construction and operation of a number of tramways in Chicago, including the famous Chicago Loop, which still operates as part of the elevated commuter railroad system today.

In September 1900 Yerkes purchased the Charing Cross, Euston & Hampstead Railway, another of the tube schemes authorized by Parliament in 1893 but which had remained moribund due to the inability of its directors to raise the necessary finance. The following year he took control of the Metropolitan District Railway and another unbuilt tube railway, the Brompton & Piccadilly Circus Railway (B&PCR). This latter line was to be merged with a fourth purchase, the Great Northern & Strand Railway, and a Bill was deposited with Parliament for consideration in 1902 which authorized a new section of line between Piccadilly Circus and Holborn that would do just that. Also in 1902, Yerkes purchased the partially built Baker Street & Waterloo Railway. All were placed within the ownership of the Underground Electric Railways Company of London (UERL), which Yerkes established in 1902.

By all accounts, Yerkes was an impressive character with excellent business acumen – tempered, of course, by some of the creative financial methods that he used. He created two separate companies in London to raise the finance for the construction and electrification of the railways that he had purchased, and stared down the formidable Metropolitan Railway in a long-running battle over the type of electrification to be used on the MR and MDR which, since they shared tracks, had to be a common system. Much of the finance was raised in the USA, through the Old Colony Trust Company of Boston, and the New York firm of Speyer & Co. The English branch of Speyer was also involved, with their London-based partner Edgar Speyer being a key player in this work.

The stories of the London tube lines that Yerkes built are in the following chapters. Sadly, Yerkes never saw any of them open. He died (probably of kidney disease) aged 68 on 29 December 1905 in the Waldorf-Astoria Hotel in New York, leaving behind a reasonable sum of money but also many debts, including to the UERL. He was replaced as Chairman of the UERL by Edgar Speyer, a financier who had been instrumental in raising the necessary funds to build the three tube railways. Sir George Gibb was appointed as Deputy Chairman and Managing Director.

Charles Yerkes was an imposing figure by the time he came to London, with a large white moustache. He was 63 years old when he began to purchase the tube railways, and many men in his position would have retired to enjoy their fortunes. Yerkes was a workaholic though, and saw the challenge of London's tube railways as the next stage of his career.

The Morgan Tubes

Charles Yerkes was not the only American financier promoting tube railways in London in the early years of the twentieth century. John Pierpont Morgan (the same Morgan whose name adorns a number of global financial institutions) was also looking at the possibility of making a handsome return by investing in the construction of London tube railways.

Morgan's interest started in late 1900, when Clinton Dawkins, a senior partner at the merchant bank, persuaded him to take an interest in the Piccadilly & City Railway. This was a railway designed to link the Brompton & Piccadilly Circus Railway (as yet unacquired by Yerkes) from its Piccadilly Circus terminus with the North East London Railway at Cannon Street. The NELR was also supported by Morgan, and together the three railways would have formed a continuous route. This would have started at South Kensington, and followed the line of the Brompton Road and then Piccadilly, before curving south to Charing Cross. It would then have taken the line of the Strand and Fleet Street, passing Ludgate Circus, to reach Cannon Street and the City. The NELR section would take the line of Gracechurch Street, curving northwards to Liverpool Street and thereafter following the Kingsland Road. At Stoke Newington it would split, with separate branches serving Tottenham and Walthamstow, which were both seen as prime locations for commuters to live.

John Pierpont Morgan

Facing page Following the amalgamation of the various railways that formed Morgan's syndicate, the promotors of what had become the London Suburban Railway published this map to show how they proposed a cohesive group of railways that would provide useful connections with the London United Tramways in west London, and would be more direct than the existing main-line railway routes serving the eastern suburbs. The large estates being planned by the London County Council are prominently marked, as it was hoped that these would bring lucrative passenger traffic to the line. The planned branch to Walthamstow has now been dropped.

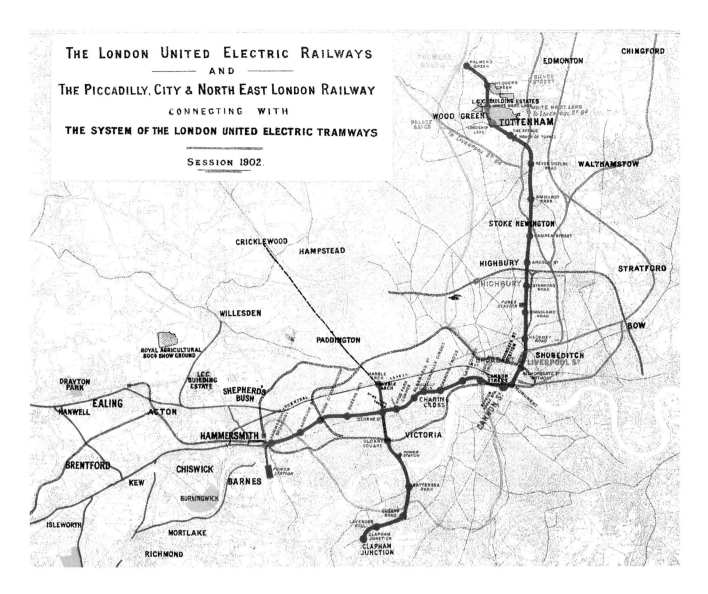

The London United Electric Railways

AND

The Piccadilly, City & North East London Railway

CONNECTING WITH

The System of the London United Electric Tramways

SESSION 1902.

Bills for the P&CR and NELR were deposited with Parliament in late 1900 for consideration in the 1901 Session. However, the opening of the Central London Railway in July 1900 had spurred a number of engineers and speculators to create new schemes, and Parliament had 14 tube railway bills to consider. To ensure that they were reviewed consistently, they appointed a Joint Select Committee (i.e., one with members from both the House of Commons and the House of Lords).

Problems appeared for Morgan and his fellow promoters with the purchase of the B&PCR in 1901 by Yerkes. The B&PCR had, in 1900, proposed an extension north-eastwards to Angel, and were objecting to the P&CR plans for an end-on junction of tunnels to allow a through service, as this would interfere with the route to Angel. The P&CR argued that their proposal would allow direct trains to the City (instead of passengers having to change onto the CLR at a proposed interchange station at Holborn).

By the time the Joint Select Committee reported, it was too late to proceed with any of the Bills, and Parliament agreed to carry them over to the 1902 Session. This did not preclude new schemes from being introduced, and by the end of 1901, there were 27 Bills covering 13 separate tube railway proposals. Morgan had added another of these to his stable, this being the City & North East Suburban Electric Railway, planned to link the City of London with Waltham Abbey. The promoters of the C&NESER had originally worked with the Chairman of the MDR, but Yerkes had refused to allow any financial support – this had led them to turn to Morgan instead.

The House of Lords created two Committees in 1902 to consider the various tube railways being proposed. That chaired by Lord Windsor considered the predominately east-west railways, and included all the lines mentioned so far in this chapter. By now, the B&PCR had had second thoughts on their Angel extension proposal, and were instead promoting a connection to Charing Cross; from here, their trains would continue eastwards on an authorized (but unbuilt) deep-level line beneath the District Railway. Additionally, they proposed the connection between Piccadilly Circus and Holborn that allowed their route to connect with the Great Northern & Strand Railway (GN&SR), as mentioned previously.

The P&CR amalgamated with the NELR in April 1902, to form the Piccadilly, City & North East London Railway. It gave up its plans for connecting with the B&PCR, and instead joined forces with a new scheme for 1902, called the London United Electric Railway. The LUER was being promoted by the London United Tramways group, and was to bring passengers from their tram terminus at Hammersmith as far as Charing Cross. A separate line from the LUER was to connect Marble Arch and Clapham Junction, with passengers changing trains between the two at Knightsbridge. Morgan bought a half-share in the LUER, and the combination of the PC&NELR, C&NESER, and LUER was known as the London Suburban Railway (LSR), and totalled 38 route-miles. The section between Hammersmith and the City, via Piccadilly Circus, also guaranteed that there would be a bitter fight with the Yerkes-backed MDR and B&PCR.

And so it proved to be. Before the Select Committee, the LSR argued that the B&PCR was only being promoted to thwart other proposals. To counter this, work was immediately started on the line, with shafts being sunk at the site of Knightsbridge station. The MDR argued that the route of the B&PCR had already been authorized, and that there was no need for any other line along this route.

The initial result of the Committee's deliberations was partial success for Morgan. Most of the LUER and PC&NELR were approved (a loop between Hammersmith and Shepherd's Bush, and the northern end of the route at Southgate were deleted). The entire Bill for the C&NESER was withdrawn after the Committee rejected the southern section of the C&NESER, as it largely duplicated the PC&NELR. A stipulation was made that the whole of the scheme had to be constructed; there was to be no 'cherry-picking' by the promoters.

On the route promoted by Yerkes, the B&PCR extension to Charing Cross was rejected on engineering grounds. The gradients and curves were extreme, and the Board of Trade's Inspector of Railways strenuously objected, threatening a 12 mph speed restriction throughout the section if it was built. The connection with the GN&SR was approved, giving Yerkes a line from Earl's Court through to Finsbury Park.

The result of this was that the Committee had approved two parallel routes between Knightsbridge and Piccadilly Circus. The Bills now returned to Parliament for the remainder of the approvals process, and the arguments continued from both sets of promoters. Other bodies submitted their objections and amendments to all of the railways, but this was not to be the cause of Morgan's failure.

Things were not completely happy within the LSR grouping. The original agreement had split the ownership and control, with Morgan holding five-eighths and the London United Tramways the remainder. The latter felt that they should have an equal share with Morgan, despite the LUER being a significantly smaller component of the whole. They argued that their tramways would bring many passengers onto the railway, and also that their company would bring its expertise in managing transport operations. Morgan refused to negotiate, and after a few days of solicitors' letters passing back and forth, the Chairman of the LUT sold his entire holding in the tramway company. This would not necessarily have been an issue for Morgan, except that they were sold to the English finance house that was supporting Yerkes.

The immediate effect was the withdrawal of the LUER parts of the Bill by the LUT's new management. The House of Lords was most displeased, feeling that this was a breach of faith with both the promoters of the P&CR, and also with Parliament. The stipulation made by the Select Committee would not now be met, and so the entire scheme collapsed. Various attempts were made to rescue the scheme, but to no avail. Yerkes had come out on top, although the press of the day wrote that it was the result of "a very dishonourable transaction", "a scandal which probably had no precedent", and "a very pretty and clever piece of manœuvring".

The Bakerloo Tube

It is rumoured that the origin of the Baker Street and Waterloo Railway (BS&WR) lies in the desire of a group of businessmen to get from their offices in Westminster to the cricket ground at Lord's. Whatever the motivations though, the line was promoted in 1892, as part of a small flurry of tube railways that hoped to ride on the success of the City & South London Railway. It was to link the two points in its name, with the section south of Westminster giving the line the potential for more traffic from passengers inter-changing at Waterloo station. This section also provided access to a site for a convenient depot, the route north of the Thames being too built up to provide a convenient location. To minimize costs, the railway followed the line of the streets above, avoiding passing beneath private property and therefore needing to purchase the freeholds. This explains the curving, slightly circuitous route that the line takes today.

A horse bus service ran between Baker Street and Waterloo at the time that the Baker Street and Waterloo Railway was promoted. The route was converted to motor bus operation in November 1904 with a 24-seater Daimler double decker providing an hourly service with a journey time of just under 30 minutes.

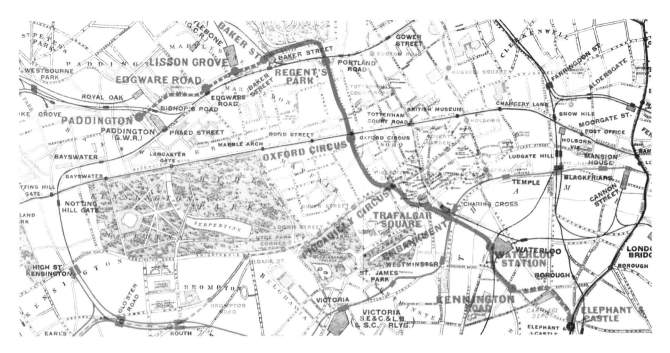

London is rapidly duplicating itself—underground. The millions who tread its busy streets day by day, and wonder at the sight of a great city's traffic, would be more amazed still could they see the confusion and complications underneath. The new "twopenny tube" will add one more to London's underground marvels. The Waterloo to Baker Street "tube," which has been building three years, and will be finished in two more, is five miles long. There will be stations at Paddington, Dorset Square, Baker Street, Oxford Circus, Piccadilly Circus, Charing Cross, the Embankment, Waterloo, and the Elephant and Castle, all these stations communicating with the stations now existing at these various places. The railway is built in the solid London clay, except about 500ft. under the bed of the Thames, which is constructed under compressed air (averaging about two atmospheres), and is in ballast. The depth from the rails to the surface of the roads varies from 7oft. at Baker Street to about 90ft. at Piccadilly Circus. The up and down lines are in separate tunnels about 12ft. diameter. The stations are built of cast iron segmental rings, similar to the running tunnels.

This map was included in the line's opening brochure, showing the extent of the service at commencement. Lisson Grove station was renamed Great Central before it opened in March 1907.

Left Press cutting prior to opening of the line.

Following approval of the original Bill for the line, little happened whilst the promoters sought to raise the necessary finance by selling shares in the company. A short extension from Baker Street to the new terminus of the Great Central Railway at Marylebone was successfully promoted in 1896, and the following year the money was forthcoming from a mining finance company. Like the C&SLR, the construction work started from a wooden platform constructed in the Thames, immediately upstream of the Charing Cross railway bridge.

The tunnels were dug by hand, from within the safety of Greathead tunnelling shields. The tunnels were continued through the site of each station to enable continuity of the work; once the shield had moved on, a short section of the cast-iron tunnel lining at one end of the future platform tunnel was dismantled, and the tunnel enlarged by hand. A larger Greathead shield was built into this section, and driven forward for the length of the platform, taking down the smaller lining as it progressed and building a larger lining behind it.

One of the most difficult parts of the construction was beneath the Thames. Survey work performed before construction started showed the presence of a large dip in the clay of the river bed, filled with waterlogged gravel – possibly the remains of dredging carried out in the 1860s for an earlier, uncompleted Waterloo & Whitehall Railway. A special shield was employed to drive the BS&WR through the gravel, and the work was carried out using airlocks and compressed air to help hold back the water. If the pressure was not judged correctly, the air would bubble through the gravel into the river, causing waterspouts! A decompression chamber was provided for the tunnellers in case they were afflicted by the 'bends', from working in the compressed air, and the company also provided medical staff, changes of clothes, and hot coffee – high standards of welfare for the day.

Tunnelling continued until late 1900, when the mining company financing the line collapsed, at which point it slowed, almost to a halt. It was not until early 1902, when Yerkes completed his purchase of the company, that the tunnelling was able to resume at pace. A southern extension had been approved by this time – just before the mining company's problems emerged – taking the line from Waterloo to Elephant & Castle. This would enable interchange with the C&SLR, as well as provide a more convenient site for the depot near to St George's Circus.

One of the consequences of the Yerkes acquisition of the BS&WR was a change in the station décor. The new owner, the UERL, decided to give each station a unique coloured tiling pattern, described in more detail in chapter 11. This left the BS&WR with a small quirk, which remained in place until retiling in 1982. The northbound platform, and some of the passageways at Trafalgar Square station (now part of Charing Cross) had been tiled, using the plain white tiles typical of the existing tube railways, probably before the change of ownership. The rest of the station was given the coloured tiles in line with other UERL stations, and this discrepancy was left to intrigue eagle-eyed passengers.

Another oddity of the line is its name. *Bakerloo* is a contraction of the line's formal name, allegedly coined (as Baker-loo) by G. H. F. Nicols, a writer for the *Evening News* in its edition of 7 March 1906. In an article noting the public opening of the line just three days later, the hyphen had been dropped, and the name was truly born. It might have remained in the pages of the newspaper, but instead the company adopted it officially in July 1906. Signs soon began to appear with the new name around the stations. *The Railway Magazine* and its editor were not impressed, noting that a railway company should not adopt its "gutter title", and that its officers were expected to have "more dignity".

The steel bodied trains for the line were all made in the USA by The American Car &

LONDON :

THE BAKER-LOO.

Trial Trip of Baker-street and Waterloo Railway.

FIRST STRAPHANGER.

London's latest 'Tuppenny Tube"—the Baker-street and Waterloo Railway—to-day carried its first passengers, and on Saturday will be open to the public.

The new line forms an important link in the elaborate system of "tube" electric railways, which, when all are completed, will give London the most modern and complete scheme of underground inter-communication in the world.

To-day an "Evening News" representative was permitted to travel on the new railway, now nearing completion after eight years' work.

The cars will be lighted by twenty incandescent sixteen-candle power lamps. The maximum speed of the trains is thirty-five miles an hour, and during trial trips which have been made over the system during the past week ... the working and acceleration of the trains have been found very smooth. In the early morning and at night there will be a five minute service; during the busy part of the day a three minute service.

Extracted from *The Scotsman*, 5 March 1906

TUBE-TRIP.

Possible Danger to be Care-fully Guarded Against.

Everyone who may travel by one of the Tube railways—and who in London may not?—should remember the following golden rule :—

Be careful when alighting from, or entering, a "tube" electric train, more especially if the station is on a curve, as is the case at many points on London's new railways.

Between the edge of the platform and the exit and entrance gates of the corridor carriages there is often a gap of several inches, into which the foot of the unwary might slip with disastrous consequences if the train suddenly started.

This need for care is particularly noticeable at the Baker-street Station on the latest "tube."

"This matter has had our most earnest consideration, and we have spared no money or time to solve the problem satisfactorily," said Mr. Chapman, of the Engineers' Department of the Baker-street and Waterloo Railway, to an "Evening News" representative.

"You will find this gap on all 'snaky railways,' where stations have to be built on a curve; the Bank Station of the Central London Railway is an example.

"Although the railway lines necessarily curve, the carriages being long and straight cannot twist or give, except where they are coupled.

"The consequence is that at certain points the saloon carriages swing out a few inches at the ends when the train is at rest in the station.

"On the Underground Railway the problem has been solved by adding a step, but on the tube railways this is impossible, owing to the lack of space in the tunnels.

"To make the tunnels larger would add enormously to the already huge cost of construction, and to make the carriages shorter and with more joints would be very inconvenient and add prohibitive amounts to our bills for wages, for there must be an attendant at each gate to let passengers in and out.

"The cause of the difficulty is this :—You cannot build a straight railway under a crooked city like London.

"Landlords and householders object to 'tubes' under their premises, and so we have to follow the curves of the twisting London thoroughfares underground.

"We would like to build stations on the straight—it would be cheaper and better; but we must have stations at points where the public want them, hence the curving stations.

THE NEW TUBE

TO-DAY'S OPENING

FEATURES AND ADVANTAGES

Kennington	depart	1 p.m
Waterloo		1 1.30 sec.
Embankment		1 3
Trafalgar Square		1 4.30 sec.
Piccadilly Circus		1 5.30 sec.
Oxford Circus		1 6
Regent's Park		1 8.30 sec.
Baker Street	arrive	1 12

The foregoing will be the timetable for the first public train over the new Baker-street and Waterloo Railway today. The fare will be 2d. all the way or to any station.

The formal opening will take place at half-past twelve, when Sir Edwin Cornwall, chairman of the London County Council, accompanied by many members of the council and other public men, with leading officials of the new railway, will enter the special train which is to run over the line with the party from Kennington to Baker-street, arriving there 12:45 p.m. The party will then proceed to the Great Central Hotel, where there will be a banquet in honour of the event.

For three weeks past trains have been running over the whole extent of the system, the uniformed conductors faithfully calling out the station, throwing open and shutting the car-gates, ringing the signal-bell, and closing the inside doors just as if each car were crowded with passengers. The staff is now perfect in its duties, and yesterday scores of trains ran backwards and forwards without a hitch of any kind. The automatic regularity of train is a pleasing feature of the service; and six minutes from Waterloo to Oxford-circus, the officials say, ought to meet the requirements of the public very satisfactorily.

The line is 35ft below the bed of the Thames, but even in this low lying portion the air is cool and sweet. The depth at Waterloo station from the booking-office level to the lower rails is 155 feet, but the terrors of ascent and descent are done away with by the magnificent service of lifts. The stairway at Waterloo has 117 steps, debouching on a long, easy slope down to the platforms, through a tunnel lined with dazzling white tile picked out in pleasing fashion with green.

Last night the finishing touches were being given at all the stations along the line. At Waterloo, which is a modern model passenger station, three public telephones are among the many conveniences at the disposal of the passengers.

STATIONS OF DIFFERENT COLOURS.

The new tube is unsurpassed for comfortable accommodation and elegance of appointments. There is a perfect flood of light, as the tube is illuminated brilliantly all the way every few yards, with electric light, and the interior lighting is splendid. The carriages are of steel and fire-resisting wood. A complete telephone system is carried out the whole length of the railway with connections even to the moving trains.

The stations are exceedingly pretty with artistic designs in coloured tiles, each station having its own distinctive tint, as:

KENNINGTON. – Dark purple arches with cream tiles in the interspaces.
WATERLOO. - Green and white.
EMBANKMENT. – Brown arches with cream and Nile green between.
TRAFALGAR-SQUARE. – The down side entirely white; the upside green arches with white between.
PICCADILLY CIRCUS. – Blue, with green and yellow
OXFORD CIRCUS. – Green and yellow
REGENT'S PARK. – Dark brown, with pale yellow between stop
BAKER-STREET. – Blue arches, with power yellow between.

Passengers will soon learn to distinguish the stations by the colours, without depending upon the names set in contrasting colours in the sides of the stations. As the Baker-street and Waterloo Railway begins business at 5.30 a.m., and runs trains at very short intervals until 12:30 midnight, both the early workman and the late theatre-goer and attender of social events will be well served.

Daily Mail, 10th March 1906. The station at Kennington Road (today's Lambeth North) has been shown as Kennington.

Foundry Company, and shipped in kit form to Manchester. Here they were assembled and then brought by main-line railway to Camden goods depot, before being pulled on wagons by horses through the central London streets at night to the depot at London Road, near Elephant & Castle.

The line remained underused for its first few months, with trains being reduced in length to cut costs. Competition from the new motor buses, together with the stark fact that the line did not connect any key traffic centres was probably the cause. The initial flat fare of 2d was soon dropped, with 1d fares for shorter distances and 3d fares for longer introduced, and passenger numbers improved.

Baker Street Station, (Baker-Loo Tube)

Above This postcard shows Baker Street station just after opening, as evidenced by the poster stuck to the façade to the left of the doors, and the large map at first-floor level. The postcard caption also uses the short-lived, hyphenated form of the name (Baker-Loo). This building was on Upper Baker Street, almost opposite Melcombe Street, and is typical of the stations designed by the architect Leslie Green.

Left In a photo from an article in the Tramway & Railway World published at the time of the line's opening, a gateman can be seen between two of the 'cars'. Carriages on the Yerkes tubes were referred to thus as an import from America, the home of the financiers and the engineers who built and equipped it.

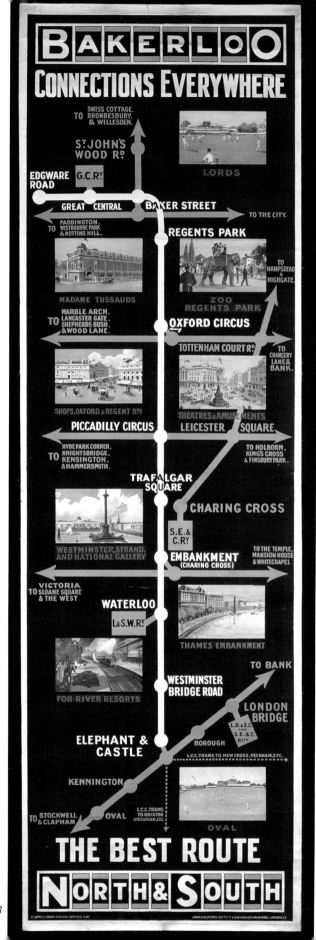

Above Part of the cover of the first map published by the BS&WR for issue to the public, showing the mixed typographic style common at the time. Like the CLR, it initially had a flat 2d fare for all journeys. A slight discount was available for multiple purchases, with 25 tickets available for 4 shillings (48d), effectively giving one free journey. Today the journey time between Baker Street and Waterloo is slightly quicker, at 10 minutes (or 7–8 minutes by Jubilee line).

Left This 1908 poster emphasized the connections that the Bakerloo made with other Underground lines, whilst portraying it as a fast, straight route across the capital. In reality, the curves that it follows restrict the speed of trains along much of its route.

This photograph from a contemporary German newspaper shows one of the Bakerloo Line platforms at Embankment. The tiling pattern used at the UERL stations is clearly visible, together with an *Art Nouveau* ventilation grille above. The tunnel portal has fake voussoir stones around it, which was also standard for these stations. Beyond the portal the tunnel is slightly enlarged for a short distance, this allowing space for the electrical cables on the tunnel wall to be switched from one side of the tunnel to the other as they passed through the platform area. A poster on the end wall warned passengers and staff of the danger of trespassing on the tracks or entering the tunnels.

A photograph of one of the cars used on the BS&WR, with the driving cab at the front. Behind is the equipment compartment, with a louvered panel providing ventilation to the motors and switchgear. The remainder of the car is the passenger compartment.

A view of the London Road depot of the BS&WR, showing a number of trains on the sidings. The cars were delivered by road from Camden, pulled by horses, and entered the depot via the long ramp seen on the left. The wooden structure at the end of the ramp was used for lifting the car bodies onto their bogies, which would have been placed on the tracks in readiness.

The Piccadilly Tube

The curving path of today's Piccadilly line across central London is a legacy of its origins, its tube section being a combination of three separately planned railways. The westernmost part was planned by the shallow Metropolitan District Railway as a deep-level alternative, to relieve congestion in their steam-hauled trains between Earl's Court and Mansion House. Parliament authorized this scheme in 1897, but the often-impoverished MDR failed to raise the capital for the new tube line.

In the same year, a new tube railway between South Kensington and Piccadilly Circus was also approved by Parliament in the same year, as the Brompton & Piccadilly Circus Railway (B&PCR). Again, funds were not forthcoming, and in 1898 the scheme was acquired by the MDR. The following year the two companies successfully promoted a Bill in Parliament joining the two tube railways at South Kensington, and giving the B&PCR the rights to construct the deep-level District tube from there to the surface, west of Earl's Court.

PROPOSED NEW UNDERGROUND RAILWAY IN LONDON.

A project is under consideration for a new line from Holborn-circus to Piccadilly ; and in due course a Bill will be introduced to Parliament authorising the scheme. The promoters' plans (the *Daily News* says) comprise two lines, both starting from Aldgate, and one proceeding along Cheapside to some point near the General Post Office. Thus far, it will be a double-track line ; but from the Post Office it will go as a four-track railway westward through Newgate-street, along Holborn, Oxford-street, and Bayswater-road to some point in the extreme west of London. The second line, starting from Aldgate, will be carried as a double line only through the City, Fleet-street, the Strand, along Piccadilly to the Green Park, and thence as a four-track railway to Knightsbridge, Kensington, and Hammersmith. At various points there will be intersecting lines, one of which will run along Shaftesbury-avenue from Oxford-street to Piccadilly. The plans are being prepared for the whole of these lines ; but the present purpose of the promoters is limited to Holborn, Oxford-street, and Shaftesbury-avenue, the proposed line terminating, as it has been said, at Holborn - circus in one direction, and Piccadilly-circus in the other. If carried out, this new line will be a novelty in London, in that it will be an electric railway. The complete design is for the laying down of four lines of rail—an up-and-down line outside for stopping trains, and an inner up-and-down line for express trains, which would stop only at important points, and would travel between the City and the extreme west of London at the rate of forty miles an hour.

Right This map was produced by the promoters of the Brompton & Piccadilly Circus Railway, and shows a number of other railways that were planned or in progress. The B&PCR is the bold red line from South Kensington to Piccadilly Circus (terminating a little further west than the current platforms at the latter station). In purple is the Central London Railway, with today's Lancaster Gate station shown as 'Westbourne'. The Bakerloo is in green and the District in brown (a reversal of the current Underground diagram), and the proposed City & West End Railway is shown in pale brown from the west (with a station at Albert Hall), running on the same route as the B&PCR to Piccadilly Circus, and then continuing eastwards to Charing Cross and beyond.

The final part of the line was promoted as the Great Northern & Strand Railway (GN&SR) in 1899. Its northern terminus was to be at Wood Green, and it was planned to run beneath the tracks of the Great Northern Railway (which gave it tacit support) to King's Cross, south of which it would run to Holborn and then on to a station at Wych Street. In September 1901, the company was purchased by Yerkes, who had also bought the MDR in March of the same year.

This would give him the ability to extend the B&PCR to the east without having to plan anything more than a short line to link the two railways. It was not possible to connect their planned termini, and so the connection with the GN&SR was to be made at Holborn, leaving the original route to Wych Street as a short branch. The Great Northern Railway insisted that the GN&SR be abandoned north of Finsbury Park as part of the deal and Wood Green was not reached by the tube until 1932.

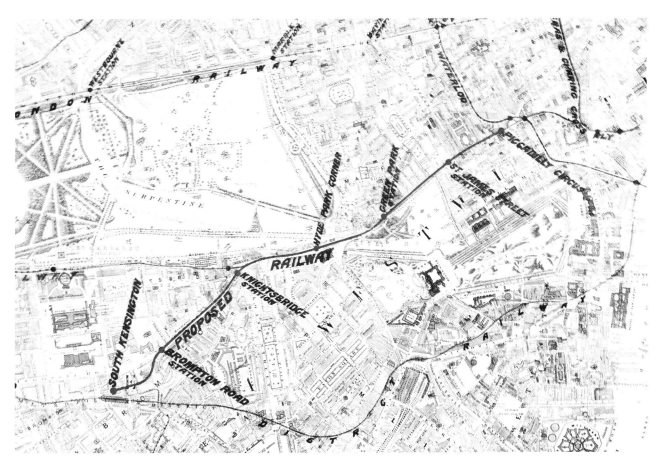

THE·BOOKING·OFFICE· PICCADILLY·STATION

MAP·OF·ROUTE

HAMMERSMITH WEST KENSINGTON EARLS COURT GLOUCESTER ROAD STH. KENSINGTON BROMPTON RD KNIGHTSBRIDGE HYDE PARK CORNER DOWN ST DOVER ST PICCADILLY CIRCUS LEICESTER SQ COVENT GARDEN

FINSBURY PARK GILLESPIE ROAD HOLLOWAY ROAD CALEDONIAN RD YORK RD KINGS CROSS RUSSELL SQUARE HOLBORN

ONE·OF·THE· CARRIAGES

LEICESTER·SQ· STATION

A·DRIVER

DRAWN BY HOWARD PENTON   FROM SKETCHES BY F. C. DICKINSON

In summary, the plans for 1902 consisted of the takeover of the GN&SR by the B&PCR, the renaming of the company as the Great Northern, Piccadilly & Brompton Railway (GNP&BR), the connecting line from Holborn to Piccadilly Circus, and (promoted by the GNR), a new station at Finsbury Park.

With the financial backing of Yerkes, construction work started in September 1902. The line was divided into three separate contracts: from the west end, to South Kensington; South Kensington to Holborn; and Holborn to Finsbury Park. The station tunnels at the latter station were constructed by the GNR, and as a result were given plain white tiling.

The District still harboured ambitions to build their deep-level tube line, and so junction tunnels were formed at South Kensington to facilitate its eventual connection, with the station platforms being at different levels to avoid the need for any tracks to cross. A short length of the westbound platform tunnel was also constructed for the deep-level District, probably to prevent damage occurring to the lift shafts had it been built at a later date.

The biggest problem faced by the company was the branch at Holborn. A variety of plans in the archives show that the manner by which the tracks would be connected to the main line, and the arrangement of the

platforms, was repeatedly revised. Delays were also caused by the London County Council (LCC), which had cleared the slums south of Holborn and were busy building a new street called Kingsway. The LCC wanted to control the look of the buildings, particularly around the crescent-shaped block formed between the Strand and Aldwych. The railway company wanted to extend the branch southwards to Waterloo, to increase its usefulness, but only as a single line. Objections to the single line caused Parliament to strike out this part of the plan, leaving a branch terminus on the south side of the Strand rather than just north of Aldwych as had been planned in 1899.

Facing page This attractive page of illustrations from the *Illustrated London News* shows views of a platform and train interior. The map is neatly wrapped around the detailed drawing of the station booking office, and the depiction of the driver shows the Spartan interior of a train cab. The drivers worked a ten-hour day, without formal meal-breaks; they brought food with them and ate when the opportunity arose, such as when the train waited briefly at a terminus.

Above In a photograph from the Piccadilly Tube's 1906 opening brochure, a typical booking hall on the Yerkes tubes is shown shortly before the line's opening.

Much of the line was tunnelled using Greathead shields, but one of the contractors introduced a shield with a rotating mechanical cutter at the front to speed up the work. The Price Rotary Excavator had been tried previously on the Central London Railway, but an improvement in the drive mechanism made the version used for the Piccadilly tube rather more successful.

The public began to use the new line on 15 December 1906. The branch to the Strand was not complete, and neither were three other stations (at South Kensington, Down Street, and Covent Garden). From the outset the line was promoted as the Piccadilly Tube, its company name being too much of a mouthful for public use. Unlike the Bakerloo line, fares were graduated from the start, and it was possible to buy tickets giving interchange with other lines.

These two cartoons as well as the full page article opposite show the interest in what the GNP&BR would be called, following the adoption of the Bakerloo name earlier in the year. The full name of the company, as shown along the side of the car in the upper photograph, was too much of a mouthful. The top cartoon provides a selection of (appalling) names, thankfully none of which were adopted. The list in the cartoon caption is: Piccaloo, Picton, Pic-a-brum, Hammerdilly, P.E.R. (Piccadilly Electric Railway) and Presto-dilly. How some of these were arrived at (even if in jest) is a mystery. Instead, the company and the public rapidly chose and stuck with the Piccadilly Tube, this being both short and distinctive.

THE NEW TUBE.

DAME LONDON: "What shall we call your little brother?"
The favourite names, as disclosed in the "Evening News" discussion, were Piccaloo, Picton, Pic-a-brum, Hammerdilly, P.E.R., and Presto-Dilly.

THE MULTIPLICITY OF TUBES.

We have the Twopenny Tube, the Piccadilly Tube, and the Bakerloo, and now a Channel Tube is projected, to be followed no doubt by tubes to everywhere. Londoners will be shot to any part of the world.

What Shall We Call It?

THE OPENING OF LONDON'S NEW—BUT NICK-NAMELESS—TUBE

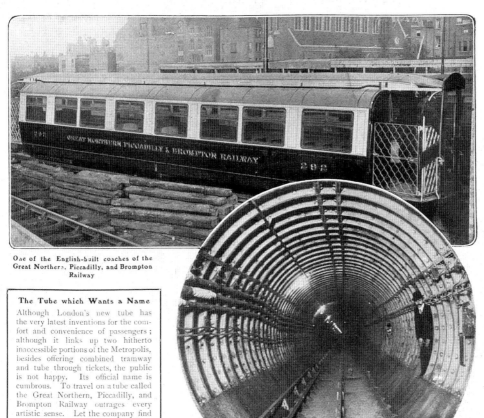

One of the English-built coaches of the Great Northern, Piccadilly, and Brompton Railway

The Tube which Wants a Name

Although London's new tube has the very latest inventions for the comfort and convenience of passengers; although it links up two hitherto inaccessible portions of the Metropolis, besides offering combined tramway and tube through tickets, the public is not happy. Its official name is cumbrous. To travel on a tube called the Great Northern, Piccadilly, and Brompton Railway outrages every artistic sense. Let the company find a portmanteau word for their line, and the public will hang on its straps with joy. Otherwise, the straps will be allowed to hang themselves

View of the "tube," showing scenery. Note man (on right) in manhole

Photos]   The interior of one of the cars. Note their comfortable strap accommodation   *[Park*

The new railway, by which Finsbury Park and Hammersmith are brought into direct communication, has just been opened for traffic

Full page feature in *The Bystander* magazine dated 19 December 1906. The cars used on the Yerkes tubes were all similar, but not identical. The photos show a single prototype car built by the Metropolitan Amalgamated Railway Carriage & Wagon Company for the Piccadilly that never ran in service. It was too big for the tunnels. The trains used were similar in design to those of the Bakerloo. However, half of them were constructed in northern France, and the other half in Hungary. They were all transported by ship to the London docks, and from there transferred by rail to the new depot at Lillie Bridge, in west London.

Great Northern, Piccadilly, & Brompton Railway.
POINTS OF INTEREST ON THE NEW ROUTE.

Above An early view of the Piccadilly Tube building at South Kensington, facing onto Pelham Street. This shows the 'house style' of the Underground Electric Railways Company of London. This building still exists, although it is no longer used for access to the station, this being via the adjacent District Railway building to the left.

Left An unusual page of advertisements for businesses along the route of the Piccadilly tube, blended with a geographically correct map on which each station name is followed by those of nearby advertisers. A single column of text at top centre gives the impression of being a newspaper article, but in reality the whole page was probably managed by the railway company and newspaper as an advert.

This map is typical of those published in newspapers by the UERL at the opening of one of their lines. Their railways are shown in bold, with all other railway lines (whether tube or main-line) being relegated to very thin lines and smaller text. The Hampstead Tube was still under construction, and the branch to Strand did not open until the end of 1907. It is unclear (perhaps an error) why Knightsbridge is shown in lighter type than all of the other Piccadilly Tube stations.

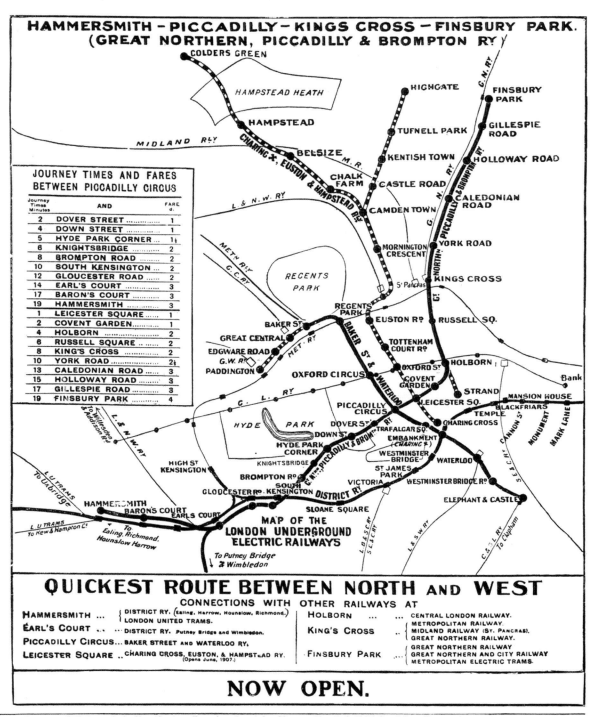

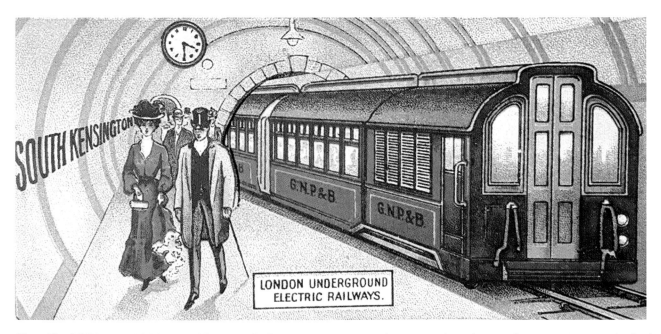

Above The UERL issued fold-out publicity cards that gave passengers information about fares and journey times on the back, together with a map of the UERL routes and places of interest nearby. The front of the card depicts a train in a platform; the train is folded over and tucks into a curved cut along the edge of the tunnel portal. There is a basic attempt to show the design of the platform, but the actual tiling pattern is absent. The tiled name, and rings of coloured tiles are more realistic. The card shown is one for the Piccadilly Tube and a similar design was issued for the Bakerloo.

PICCADILLY TUBE.

REDUCED
SEASON TICKET RATES.

RED FIGURES ARE 1 MONTH RATES.

BLACK FIGURES ARE 3 MONTH RATES.

e.g.:—King's Cross and Gloucester Road.

	1 month
8/-	
22/6	3 months

The 6, 9 & 12 Monthly Season Ticket Rates are twice three and four times the 3 monthly rates respectively.

Through Season Tickets are also issued with certain connecting Lines. Forms of application and full particulars can be obtained at any of the Company's Booking Offices.

Hammersmith.

Barons Court.	Earls Court.	Gloucester Rd.	S. Kensington.	Brompton Rd.	Knightsbridge.	Hyde Pk. Corner.	Down Street.	Dover Street.	Piccadilly Circus.	Leicester Sq.	Covent Garden.	Holborn.	Russell Square.	King's Cross.	York Road.	Caledonian Rd.	Holloway Rd.	Gillespie Rd.	Finsbury Park.
4/- 11/6																			
5/- 17/-	4/- 11/6																		
8/- 22/6	8/- 22/6	4/- 11/6																	
10/- 28/6	8/- 22/6	4/- 11/6	4/- 11/6																
10/- 28/6	8/- 22/6	4/- 11/6	4/- 11/6	4/- 11/6															
12/- 34/6	10/- 28/6	8/- 22/6	4/- 11/6	4/- 11/6	4/- 11/6														
12/- 34/6	12/- 34/6	8/- 22/6	8/- 22/6	4/- 11/6	4/- 11/6	4/- 11/6													
12/- 34/6	12/- 34/6	8/- 22/6	8/- 22/6	8/- 11/6	4/- 11/6	4/- 11/6	4/- 11/6												
12/- 34/6	12/- 34/6	8/- 22/6	8/- 22/6	8/- 22/6	8/- 17/-	4/- 11/6	4/- 11/6	4/- 11/6											
12/- 34/6	12/- 34/6	8/- 22/6	8/- 22/6	8/- 22/6	8/- 22/6	8/- 17/-	4/- 11/6	4/- 11/6	4/- 11/6										
12/- 34/6	12/- 34/6	10/- 28/6	8/- 22/6	8/- 22/6	8/- 22/6	8/- 22/6	5/- 17/-	4/- 11/6	4/- 11/6	4/- 11/6									
12/- 34/6	12/- 34/6	12/- 34/6	8/- 22/6	8/- 22/6	8/- 22/6	8/- 22/6	8/- 22/6	4/- 11/6	4/- 11/6	4/- 11/6	4/- 11/6								
12/- 34/6	12/- 34/6	12/- 34/6	8/- 22/6	8/- 22/6	8/- 22/6	8/- 22/6	8/- 22/6	8/- 17/-	5/- 11/6	4/- 11/6	4/- 11/6								
12/- 34/6	12/- 34/6	12/- 34/6	8/- 22/6	8/- 22/6	8/- 22/6	8/- 22/6	8/- 22/6	8/- 22/6	6/- 11/6	4/- 11/6	4/- 11/6	4/- 11/6							
12/- 34/6	12/- 34/6	12/- 34/6	8/- 22/6	8/- 22/6	8/- 22/6	8/- 22/6	8/- 22/6	8/- 17/-	6/- 11/6	4/- 11/6	4/- 11/6								
16/- 45/6	16/- 45/6	16/- 45/6	12/- 34/6	12/- 34/6	12/- 34/6	12/- 34/6	12/- 34/6	12/- 28/6	10/- 26/-	10/- 17/-	8/- 11/6	6/- 11/6	4/- 11/6	4/-					
16/- 45/6	16/- 45/6	16/- 45/6	12/- 34/6	12/- 34/6	12/- 34/6	12/- 34/6	12/- 34/6	12/- 34/6	12/- 28/6	10/- 22/6	8/- 22/6	8/- 11/6	4/- 11/6	4/-					
16/- 45/6	16/- 45/6	16/- 45/6	12/- 34/6	12/- 34/6	12/- 34/6	12/- 34/6	12/- 34/6	12/- 34/6	12/- 28/6	10/- 22/6	8/- 22/6	8/- 12/6	6/- 11/6	4/- 11/6	4/-				
16/- 45/6	16/- 45/6	16/- 45/6	12/- 34/6	12/- 34/6	12/- 34/6	12/- 34/6	12/- 34/6	12/- 34/6	12/- 31/6	11/- 26/-	9/- 22/6	8/- 14/6	6/- 14/6	4/- 11/6	4/-				
16/- 45/6	16/- 45/6	16/- 37/-	14/- 37/-	14/- 37/-	14/- 37/-	14/- 37/-	14/- 37/-	14/- 34/6	12/- 31/6	11/- 26/-	9/- 26/-	9/- 14/6	6/- 14/6	6/- 11/6	4/- 11/6	4/-			

PASSENGER AGENT'S OFFICE,
42. HAYMARKET, S.W.
MARCH 3rd, 1907.

Today's zonal fares are far easier to manage than the system used until the 1980s, whereby fares were based upon distance and every pair of stations had its own set of fares (for adults, children, season tickets, etc.). This table, issued by the Piccadilly Tube in March 1907 shows all of the one- and three-month season ticket rates on the line. Unlike today, there was no discount for longer periods than three months.

The Hampstead Tube

The Hampstead, St Pancras & Charing Cross Railway was promoted in Parliament in the session of 1892, along with the Waterloo & City and Baker Street & Waterloo Railways. Its name reflected its intended route from the village of Hampstead to the main-line station of Charing Cross, with a branch serving the other main-line termini of Euston, King's Cross, and St Pancras. Parliament rejected the branch beyond Euston, and hence the company was renamed the Charing Cross, Euston & Hampstead Railway (CCE&HR). Like the BS&WR, it struggled to raise the necessary funds for its construction, and lay almost dormant for the rest of the nineteenth century; only the occasional Parliamentary Bill extended deadlines. It was in 1899 that significant changes were made, firstly to place Euston on the main line, rather than on a short branch, and secondly to provide a longer branch from Camden Town to Kentish Town.

The railway might have remained unbuilt, had it not been for Yerkes. He was invited to England in 1900 by two of the promoters of the CCE&HR, and during his stay agreed to purchase the company for £100,000. It was during this time that the decision was made to extend the original line northwards to an isolated crossroads in a hamlet called Golders Green, where the land for a depot and power station would be cheaper and there was the prospect of housing being built that would accommodate new passengers for the railway. The Kentish Town branch was also extended north to the Archway Tavern in the same Bill.

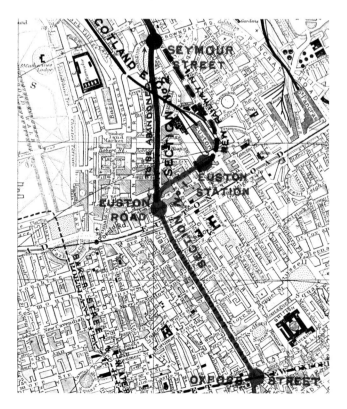

A map produced to show the change of plan for the line in the Euston area following the refusal of consent to take the planned short branch line to King's Cross due to objections from the Midland Railway, who did not want tunnelling beneath their new and massive station building at St Pancras. It made sense in the circumstances to incorporate a station at Euston on the main route instead of as part of a branch. Note the original name intended for the station at Mornington Crescent.

The residents of Hampstead protested loudly against the railway, objecting to it passing beneath Hampstead Heath, and even claiming that the tunnels would drain the water from the soil and kill the trees through vibration from the trains. However, this was easily refuted, especially as the tunnels below the Heath were (and remain) the deepest on the Underground, up to 67m below the surface. This did cause problems for the tunnellers, as the weight of the soil above broke the rotary tunnelling machines that were in use, and forced them to switch to hand mining the tunnels using Greathead shields.

The continuous climb to Hampstead had originally caused the promoters to suggest that the trains would be cable-hauled, not believing that electricity would have the power to move trains up the gradient. One of the benefits of extending the line to Golders Green was that the gradient could be reduced (as the tunnel only needed to rise to the height of the land to the north of the hill on which Hampstead is situated), although this came at the cost of increasing the depth of the platforms at Hampstead.

Another change to the early plans concerned the branch to Kentish Town and Archway Tavern, which was to have operated as a shuttle service. Passengers would have changed to trains on the main route at Camden Town. By 1903, the company was intending to run direct trains from both of the northern branches to Charing Cross, and had to spend time persuading the Board of Trade (which supervised railway safety) that the tunnel layout and signalling would prevent trains colliding at the junction. It was also due to the BoT that a low-level subway was constructed between the CCE&HR and the Central London Railway at the latter's Tottenham Court Road station, as they were worried about the potential for congestion otherwise.

The local desire to protect Hampstead Heath had one significant outcome for the line. A station was planned between Hampstead and Golders Green, with Yerkes hoping that the land around the station would rapidly fill with houses, and thus commuters. He did not reckon with Dame Henrietta Barnett, one of the driving forces behind the creation of Hampstead Garden Suburb. In order to provide more open land for the residents to enjoy, she arranged for a large amount of land to the north of the existing Heath to be purchased and set aside, protected from development. This was where the station was to be sited, and although Barnett did not object to a station (she hoped that it would help Londoners travel to enjoy the Heath at weekends), Yerkes and the CCE&HR promoters realized that it would substantially reduce the traffic prospects for the station, which would be expensive to construct given that its platforms would be over 200 feet deep. The station was not completed.

When the line opened on 22 June 1907, it was promoted as 'The Last Link', and passengers were carried free for the day. The trains were supplied by The American Car & Foundry Company, but unlike those on the Bakerloo, were built from British materials at a site in Trafford Park, Manchester, with some assembly work completed in the depot at Golders Green. They carried destination plates in their front right-hand windows; important given that the line had a choice of northern destinations. Each of the branches had a 4-minute service in the peak hours, and 5 minutes off-peak, with all trains running to Charing Cross. The line between Camden Town and Charing Cross therefore had a 2-minute peak service, falling slightly to 2½-minutes off-peak. Only one in three trains ran between Hampstead and Golders Green, reflecting the very low number of passengers originating at the terminus. Hampstead was provided with a crossover in the tunnel north of the station to allow for the remaining trains to reverse.

Posters were issued by the Hampstead Tube encouraging Londoners to move out to Golders Green (at that time spelled with an apostrophe) to enjoy healthier living, and commute to their jobs using a season ticket. By 1914, the hamlet was fast becoming a suburb, with almost ten times as many passengers (10.3 million) using the station compared to when it opened in 1907. This poster dates from 1910.

"TUBE" FREE DAY

THE OPENING OF THE NEW HAMPSTEAD LINE

Tens of thousands of Londoners will enjoy a free ride on the electric railway today. The Hampstead "Tube", reaching from Charing Cross to Golder's Green, will be opened to the public and under the novel condition that anyone who wishes to make the journey may do so without charge. The booking offices will be opened at half-past-one and the ordinary tickets to the various stations will be issued free on application.

Yesterday an army of workmen was engaged along the line putting the finishing touches to the stations; clerks were in the booking offices making themselves acquainted with tickets, while empty trains traversed the line to from end to end at intervals of a few minutes. It was the final stage of a dress rehearsal which has been going on for days.

A great rush of passengers is expected, and the company are making all preparations for a tremendous traffic. Special precautions are being taken to keep order and to guard against overwhelming pressure. Two-hundred constables will be on duty inside and outside every station and in the trains.

FREE RIDES TO GOLDER'S GREEN

Though thousands of people availed themselves of the free journey offered by the company on this the first day of the opening of the new tube, there were none of those exciting scenes which are witnessed on the occasion of the launch of similar undertakings when a prize is offered to the first passenger or the interest of the public is stimulated by some other means. There was simply a stream of passengers, as large as could be conveniently dealt with, but not large enough to get out of hand, flowing steadily the whole afternoon from the Strand into the yard of Charing-cross station, and by means of steps and lift into the trains which ran every few minutes. There could scarcely have been better afternoon to visit to the pleasant slopes of Hampstead, and some time before the line was thrown open – about one o'clock – a long queue of people was drawn up in the Strand. The free rides outward will be continued until 9.15 this evening.

The Hampstead Tube trains spent most of their lives underground, only emerging onto the surface at Golders Green station and within the adjacent depot. This photograph from *The Railway Times* shows one of the motor cars, with its cab on the right. The louvres behind the cab show the location of the equipment compartment, with the passenger area to the left. At the left-hand end, the platform and 'gate' can be seen, through which all passengers had to board and alight.

One of the non-stop trains at Golders Green station, with a very prominent headboard advertising the nature of the service.

A group of train staff posed in front of one of the trains, presumably at Golders Green depot since this was the only open-air location on the Hampstead Tube.

A year after opening, the line pioneered the use of non-stop trains on tube railways, with a service from Highgate skipping all intermediate stations before Camden Town.

In late 1909, seven non-stop services were introduced on the Golders Green branch (the apostrophe was soon dropped from the station name after it opened), running direct between Golders Green and Euston. The idea saved a few minutes, although the inability to pass a stopping service in front limited the opportunity to make significant time savings. They served a purpose though, as in various permutations they continued to operate up until the Second World War.

A quiet Golders Green station, the northern terminus at time of opening. The large building with chimneys in the background is part of the railway depot.

To increase off-peak traffic, when the tube railway had capacity to spare, the companies issued picture postcards of places that could be conveniently visited. This card, part of a series issued by the Hampstead Tube, invited people to travel to various spots in Hampstead.

The First Tube Trains

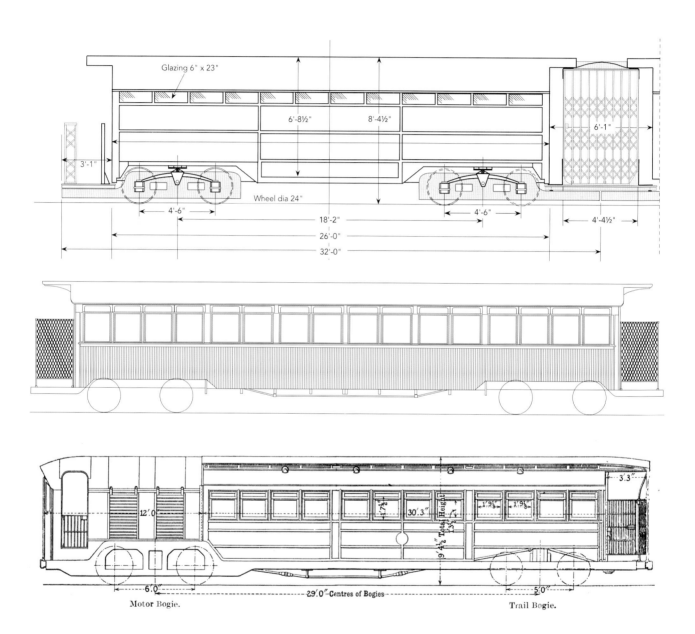

These drawings show the three designs of tube carriage introduced between 1890 and 1900. First is one for the City & South London Railway, finished in varnished wood, probably teak. The shallow windows were initially felt best for journeys all in tunnel. Second is a carriage for the Waterloo & City Railway, then owned by the London & South Western Railway. The original livery for the W&CR was brown with salmon pink window frames. The third is for the Central London Railway, painted in 'Engine Lake' (a dark red) with cream upper panels.

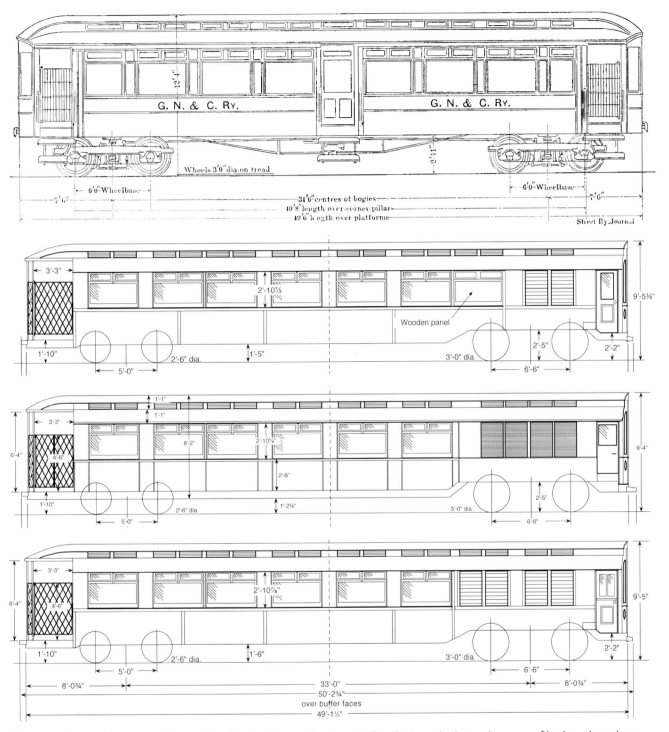

The top drawing shows a trailer carriage for the Great Northern & City Railway, built to a larger profile than the other tubes. In addition to the gates at both ends, it has a hand-operated door in the centre. The livery was varnished teak and mahogany. The other drawings show three basically similar designs for the three Yerkes tubes. In this case the motor cars are shown as it is in these that the most noticeable differences can be seen. The Bakerloo line car (first of the three) was painted in red with cream upper panels, while the Piccadilly and Hampstead cars were painted Engine Lake.

Shared Style

By the end of 1902, construction work was in progress on all three of the tubes owned by Yerkes. It is not known whether the original promoters for each of the lines had designs for their stations and equipment in mind, but once Yerkes and the UERL were in charge a common design began to take shape. For the stations, a young architect called Leslie Green was engaged by the company in September 1903. He conceived a style that could be adapted to the shape of each site, yet which would be clearly part of a common family of stations. Following modern American practice, the buildings were designed with steel load-bearing frames, allowing additional storeys to be erected on top of the buildings later, and thus bringing in rental income for the company. The stations required two-storey buildings, so that lift machine rooms could be placed on the first floor directly above the lift shafts (the exceptions being at Marylebone, where the ticket hall was in the basement and the machine rooms on the ground floor, and Waterloo, for which the building just led onto a passageway to the underground ticket hall set well back from the street). The machine rooms did not take up all of the space, and the remainder was used as office space, either by the railway company or tenants.

The walls of the station buildings were constructed from brickwork, with the main façades covered in distinctive glazed terracotta in a colour known as *sang de bœuf* or ox-blood. This was apparently chosen

because it was quick to erect and cheap to buy. Each façade was divided into a number of sections, with the precise layout depending on the length and shape of the site. There were wide openings at ground floor, used for station entrances and exits, or for small shop units, with arched windows above at first floor level. Narrower sections contained doors leading to stairs to the first floor, or blank glazed walls, with rectangular or circular windows on the upper level. Decorative mouldings were made around the window arches, and the small circular windows have heavy but decorated lintels curving over them; the small rectangular windows are rather plainer.

Most stations were given an individualistic touch through the use of cartouches placed between adjacent arches or on the building corners. Some were given particularly distinctive features, such as the pedimented window and acutely curved end to Chalk Farm building, or the UERL monogram at Oxford Circus. At Leicester Square the first floor offices were occupied by J. Wisden & Co., publishers of the cricketing 'bible', and a moulded panel featuring their name together with a set of stumps, two bats, and a ball was placed above the doorway.

The names of both the station and the railway company were placed across the façades on friezes above each floor. The style of these varied between the lines, as well as over time. The Bakerloo stations appear to have used ornate gilt lettering, displaying the name of the company below the roofline and the station name above the ground floor. The Hampstead Tube reversed the location of the information, and used black letters in a blocky style. The Piccadilly used a mixture of both, and typically enough, each line has a few exceptions.

In a photograph from the Piccadilly Tube's 1906 opening brochure, the booking hall at Brompton Road station (on the Piccadilly Tube) is shown shortly before the line's opening. This station closed in 1934, and was located between South Kensington and Knightsbridge. The decorative tiling on the walls and for the ticket office windows can be clearly seen.

Within the ticket halls, walls were tiled in bottle-green tiling from the floor up to a decorative band of tiling at head height. At most stations this featured a design based on either acanthus leaves or pomegranates, but it was plain at the last stations to be built. Cream tiling was used above this band to ceiling level with ornate glazed ceramic ticket windows in bottle green.

The most elaborate decoration was saved for the platforms and connecting passageways. Unlike the previous tube railways that used white glazed tiles to maximize the brightness of the station, given the relatively feeble electric lighting, the UERL used coloured tiles as their platforms were lit with arc lamps. Each station was given a unique combination of pattern and colour from platform to a height of about 7 ft 6 ins, broken into bays by rings of tiles that circled over the tunnel vault. At most stations three panels featured the station name, glazed into the tiles, in place of the patterns. The work involved at least 40 different tiling patterns on 94 separate platforms, covering what has been calculated as six linear miles of tiling – an incredible feat, given that every platform had a slightly different layout for its entrances, exits, and other features around which the patterns had to be fitted.

Unsurprisingly, equipment at the stations was also standardized. Ticket halls and platforms were provided with large clocks in copper cases made by the Self-Winding Clock Company of New York. Lighting was provided from Maxim arc lights fitted on brackets outside the station, in the ticket halls, and along the platforms. The lifts were made by the Otis Company, for the most part fitted in pairs in shafts of 23 ft diameter; each lift had a trapezoid floor plan, maximizing the use of space in the circular shaft.

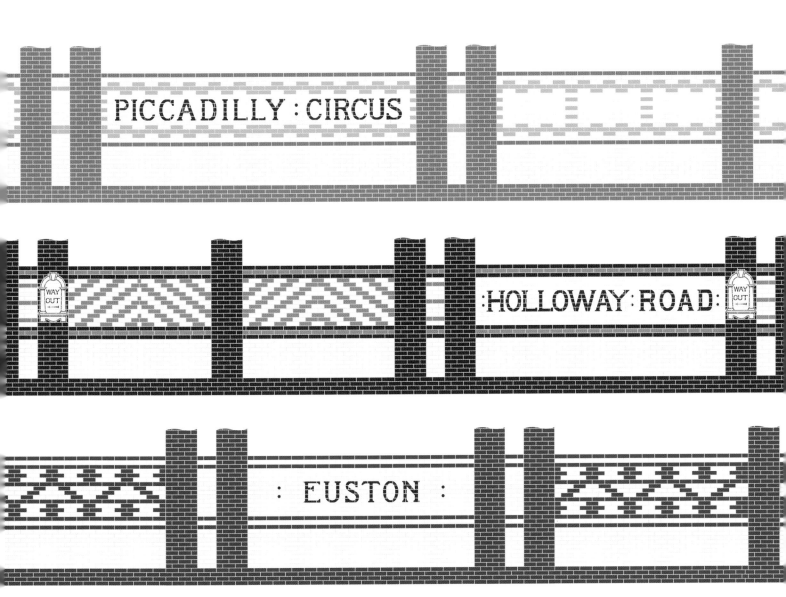

Though great play was made of the unique tile patterns in the seating bays on the Victoria Line platforms when they opened in 1968, the three Yerkes tubes preceded this feat in a far more impressive fashion over sixty years earlier, where the entire length of all platforms (except the northbound at Trafalgar Square and Strand – later Aldwych) received repeating tile patterns. There was a clear desire for a unique visual identity for every station. There were many exceptions to the various features, though a dominant standard was obvious. On the platform side were thirty courses of 9x3-inch coloured tiles punctuated by vertical 'rings' two-and-a-half tiles wide projecting over the tunnel vault and down to the trackside to train roof level, where they met a full-length continuous horizontal course of three tiles.

Above the 4-course visual plinth lower panels were in a single colour, most commonly cream or white, up to a waistband of usually three or four courses and a frieze usually mirroring it. The most common pattern panel width was 18 tiles, but with many exceptions dictated by the unique geography of every station. The patterns were applied in the upper panels, adapted to the space available. As the programme evolved, double rings were soon applied either side of the name panels to help draw attention, where previously, and on-going, they had only been used either side of doorways. There is a strong argument that the stations on the three Yerkes tubes, then operated as separate companies, were the first true example of a corporate identity on what became the London Underground.

Power supply

The electricity to power the C&SLR came from a generating station built at the line's depot in Stockwell. Six coal-fired boilers produced steam that drove three generators, each of which produced 500 volts at 450 amps (225 KW). Although very small by today's standards, at the time it was the world's largest generating station. The W&CR and CLR also built their own generating stations, at Waterloo and Wood Lane respectively.

As Charles Yerkes assembled his collection of London railways, he saw the benefits of having a single power station. This would need a large supply of cooling water, and be located somewhere that would allow vast quantities of fuel to be supplied cheaply. The economies of a single facility would be considerable though. A site was chosen in Lots Road, Chelsea, alongside the Thames, and in late 1902 work commenced. The enormous building was one of the first in Britain to use a steel frame – an example of the American methods being imported by Yerkes's team. The frame was made by a German company, and so its specification was in millimetres. Four chimneys rose to a height of 275 ft, and loading and unloading facilities for coal and ash were installed alongside Chelsea Creek. The artist James Whistler was appalled, protesting that the view of Chelsea Reach painted by Turner would be ruined.

When it opened in 1905, it was now the largest power station in the world, with 44·5 MW of generating capacity installed (almost 200 times that of the original C&SLR Stockwell power station). Not all of its power was needed at first, but as the Bakerloo, Piccadilly, and Hampstead Tubes were opened in 1906-7, more was produced. Shortcomings with the equipment meant that the original steam turbines were replaced in 1908, which also increased the maximum power to 48 MW.

The electricity was supplied at 11,000 volts via cables that led from the Lots Road power station, underneath nearby streets, to Earl's Court station. From here it was fed to a network of substations located along the three tube lines and the MDR which converted it to 630 volts DC to power the trains, and lower voltages for signalling. Many of the substations were in buildings that used polychrome brickwork in contrast to their neighbouring station buildings.

Facing page A pair of postcards issued by the Piccadilly Tube showing the exterior and interior of the power station at Lots Road, which supplied all three of the Yerkes tubes as well as the Metropolitan District Railway. Companies such as the Underground group were proud of their engineering achievements, and often published postcards of subjects that showed them 'behind the scenes'.

G.N. PICCADILLY & BROMPTON Ry.-POWER HOUSE, CHELSEA.

GREAT NORTHERN, PICCADILLY & BROMPTON Ry. POWER HOUSE, CHELSEA.

Lighting

The very first tube platforms, on the C&SLR, were not lit by electricity as might be expected, but by gas – the generating capacity of the small power station at Stockwell was insufficient to provide lighting as well as traction current. Arc lamps were provided as backup; this type of light provided the best illumination for the power available at the time. This lighting continued to be used on extensions of the line up to 1907.

The Central London Railway had more power in reserve at its generating station, and installed and used Maxim arc lights on its platforms from the opening in 1900. The lights were suspended along the centre line of the platform, and consisted of a vitreous enamelled steel casing from which a glass globe shone the light down and around; a steel disc was fitted just above the globe to reflect more light downwards. Power was supplied via cables that looped downwards to join a series of cables running along the platform wall, as can be seen in the photos on pages 16 and 17. The same type of lights were used on the Great Northern & City Railway, and a contemporary postcard shows that a pulley arrangement allowed the lamps to be lowered for maintenance.

The three UERL tube railways opened in 1906-7. Maxim lamps were installed on the

An early photograph of the island platform at Angel station, showing an unusual mixture of gas and electric lights on the same lampposts. This view looks west towards the platform stairs in the background; to the right of the stairs a C&SLR locomotive can just be seen.

Left The entrance to Charing Cross station (now Embankment) in 1909, clearly showing one of the Maxim arc lights suspended on a bracket over the doorway.

Below The interior of one of the gate stock cars on one of the Yerkes tubes, probably the Bakerloo line, showing the line of incandescent lamps along the ceiling.

platforms, in the ticket halls, and illuminating the façades of the station buildings (as shown at South Kensington on page 47). The platform lights were provided with fittings that allowed them to be slid down the curved walls for inspection and repair. Power was supplied from the current rails at the stations, and also fed incandescent lamps at the stations. Stations also had a third set of lights, all incandescent, and powered from the local area electricity supply, thus ensuring that some lights would remain illuminated in the event of a traction power supply failure.

King's Cross station on the C&SLR, with Maxim arc lights along the ceiling.

Below The Railway Magazine was very impressed by the lighting installed in the new CLR station at Liverpool Street.

By 1909 incandescent lamps were bright enough to be used on platforms (and required less maintenance and cost less to run – a 60% saving was claimed). The arc lights in use from opening were replaced by more closely-spaced incandescent lamps with hexagonal opal glass shades. These early lamps were claimed to be of 100 candle-power brightness, and sets of probably five 100 V bulbs connected in series were powered from the 500 V lighting circuits.

SCIENTIFIC ILLUMINATION AT THE NEW LIVERPOOL STREET STATION.—CENTRAL LONDON RAILWAY.

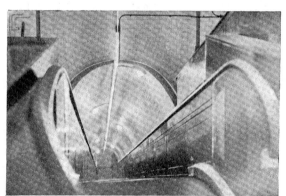

SIEMENS' SPECIAL BULKHEAD LIGHTING IN ESCALATOR TUNNEL.

BOOKING HALL UNDER THE GREAT EASTERN TERMINUS.

SUBWAY CONNECTING THE CENTRAL LONDON AND GREAT EASTERN STATIONS.

A PLATFORM AT LIVERPOOL STREET STATION, CENTRAL LONDON RAILWAY.

These installations have all been planned on a scientific basis, and the above illustrations (from photographs taken by the actual lighting) show the uniformity of illumination and complete absence of shadows.

Paddington station on the Bakerloo line was fitted with incandescent lighting from the start.

Stations were converted to incandescent lamps over the next few years, and no further arc lights were installed on new stations. The extension of the CLR to Liverpool Street in 1912 was fitted throughout with "Wotan" and "Tantalum" incandescent lamps supplied by Siemens. Glass shades made by Holophane diffused the light from the 15 Wotan lamps on each platform.

Liverpool Street station, CLR, was notable as being the first Underground station to have strip lighting – the Moore gas discharge lamp, which can be considered as an early version of the fluorescent tube. The lights were fitted centrally to the ceilings of the two escalator shafts leading down from the ticket hall at Liverpool Street main-line station as glass tubes around 90 ft long. Smaller 'bulkhead' lights, using incandescent bulbs, were provided in the escalator shafts as emergency lighting. The rapid improvements in incandescent bulbs, combined with the fragility of the glass tubes, meant that this type of lighting was not used elsewhere on the Underground until the later years of World War 2, when fluorescent lighting from the US giant GEC was introduced at Piccadilly Circus station.

The incandescent lamps and their opal glass shades lasted until 1980, when the last of their number were finally extinguished at Archway station.

Carbon filament bulbs were used on tube trains from the start. The C&SLR had just four lamps in each of its original carriages, and it was recorded that these would dim to a dull red glow as the train motors pulled as much current as they could from the rails on the arduous climb into King William Street station. Two emergency oil lamps were provided in each carriage in case of electrical failure.

The W&CR, CLR, and Yerkes tubes all provided illumination for their passengers using similar lamps, but more of them. By the time of the Yerkes tubes, 20 were reported as being in use. Emergency oil lamps were also provided, but in 1905 the CLR experimented with providing a battery to supply lighting power if the traction current failed. This was found to work, but it was not until 1914 that the Yerkes tubes followed suit.

Making a Game of It

The novelty of tube travel meant that it was not long before other businesses were trying to link themselves with the concept, with varying degrees of success. Board game manufacturers were quick off the mark, with a number of products being marketed.

The earliest game shown here is that of The Twopenny Tube, which involves three players racing between Bank and Shepherd's Bush by tube, tram, and bus. Although the routes depicted are different, there are the same number of spaces and 'stops' (at which a turn is forfeited), so the game is fair for all players – but not realistic!

A game of Yerko, from the manufacturer F. H. Ayres, is similar to a couple of modern games, in that it was based on travel around London (rather than just along a single route). Players rolled three dice: one with coloured spots, and two with conventional numbers. The die with coloured spots gave the permitted mode or modes of transport, and the player then moved their piece in accordance with the numbered dice and the rules ("For walk or motorbus moves, count sum of both numbers. For horse bus moves, count higher number of the two. For District Railway or Tube moves, count lower of the two.") The map was reasonably accurate, and the rules about moves ensured that the relative speed of travel for the different modes was represented. The map conflated the Metropolitan and District Railways to give two categories of rail travel: Tube or District.

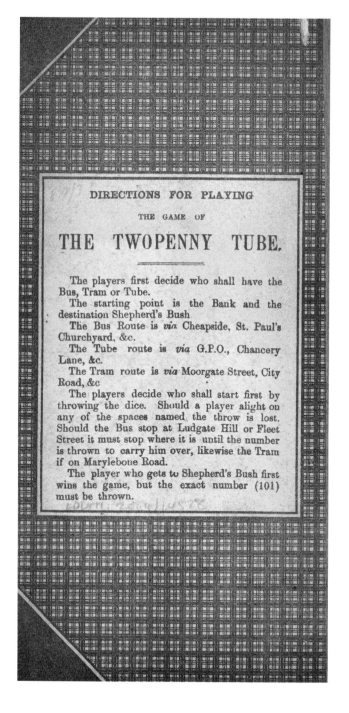

The playing board for The Twopenny Tube game

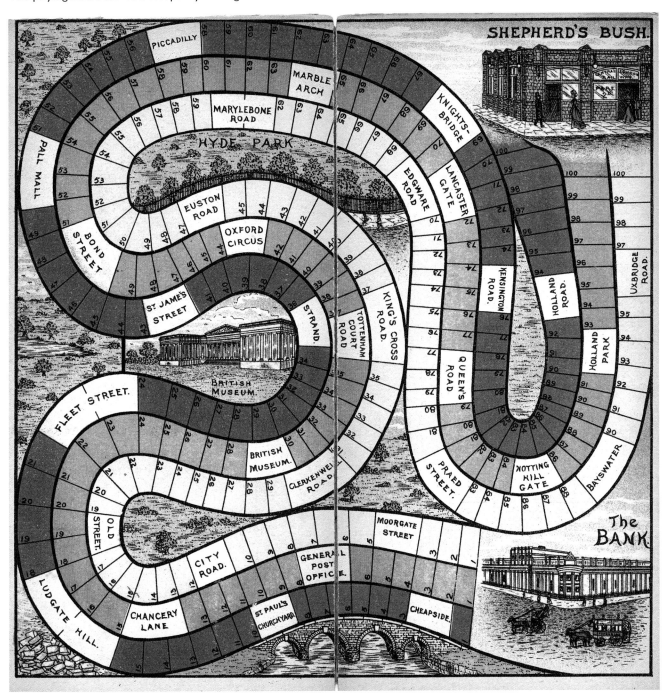

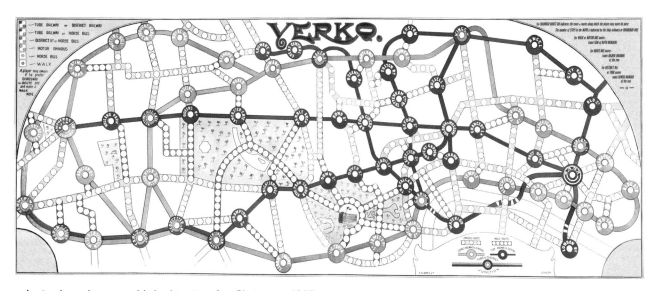

A nice board game published in time for Christmas 1907.

The cover picture on the wooden box in which the game was supplied gave the name based on ten of the station names, but the similarity to "Yerkes" cannot be a coincidence! The London *Standard* newspaper, in a review of board games for Christmas 1907, noted that

A new game which is sure to win its full measure of popularity during the Christmas holidays, especially to young Londoners, is the "London Travel" game known as "Yerko" which will supply plenty of instruction on finding one's way about by tube, bus or pedestrian route.

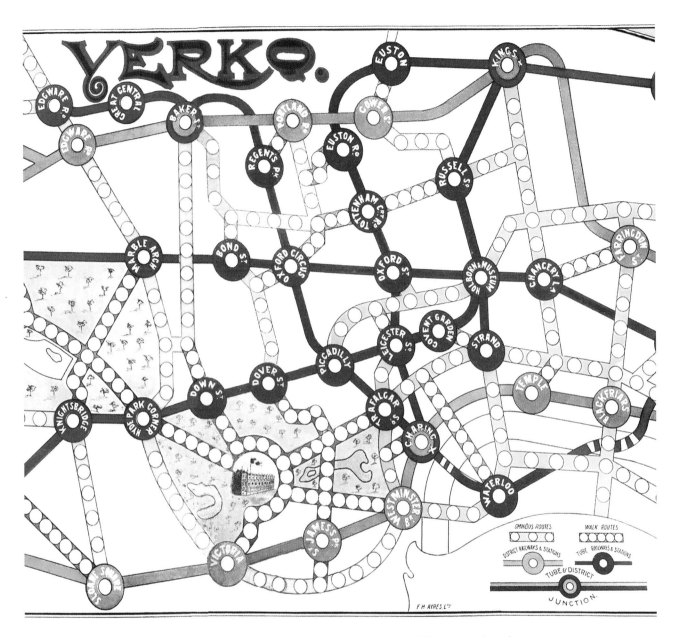

This enlargement of part of the playing board shows more clearly how the different modes of transport were distinguished. We do not have the rules of the game but the aim seems to have been to get from the left side of the board to the Bank station using the methods that were determined by the throwing of a die. The six possibilities in descending order of value were: (a) a choice of travel between District and Tube, (b) a choice between Tube and horse bus, (c) a choice between District and horse bus, (d) motor omnibus, (e) horse bus, and (f) walking.

Towards Unification

By mid-1907, all of the tube railways that had been under construction in the early 1900s had opened, and there was a growing realization that they would not turn out be the quick way to a large profit that their promoters and investors had hoped. There were few new schemes being promoted, and no new lines would be opened until the Victoria line in the late 1960s. It was time for some consolidation.

London had seven tube railways, owned by five separate companies, as well as the sub-surface Metropolitan and District Railways. The latter two, despite extensive operation over each other's tracks, had had a tempestuous relationship in the late 1800s, due to the strained relations between the chairmen of the companies. Maps produced by any of the companies highlighted their own route boldly. If the other companies' lines

Facing page In May 1907, this logo appeared in public for the first time, giving a common identity to the three tubes owned by the UERL. It was designed by W. J. Pawsey in response to a competition in the *Evening News*, but was fairly short-lived due to its replacement by the UNDERGROUND logo the following year.

Below 1908 map cover showing the first use of the Underground logotype.

were shown at all, it was in a more muted style. The exception was with the maps of the District, Bakerloo, Piccadilly, and Hampstead, which were all under the same ownership.

The lack of centralized planning and co-operation between the companies had also led to some varied interchange arrangements. The best were between lines owned by the UERL, which provided interchange passages at low-level between platforms since through ticketing was provided. Where lines owned by different companies connected, the most convenient had low-level ticket offices in the passageways – that at Euston remains, empty, in a long-disused subway. More awkwardly, passengers would have to ascend to ticket hall level to purchase an onward ticket, and the worst connections were those where separate, but nearby stations were built. Notting Hill Gate was a good example of this, with stations on opposite sides of the main road. Further east on the Central London Railway, passengers wanting the Piccadilly Tube had to alight at British Museum station, walk 170 yards along High Holborn, and cross Kingsway in order to reach Holborn station.

As early as 1907 the management of the various companies began to hold meetings to co-ordinate fares. This soon included the bus operators, and a regular London Passenger Traffic Conference was instituted, looking at fares and co-ordination of routes. Through 1908, the companies worked to establish through ticketing (i.e., a ticket purchased from a station owned by one company would be valid for travel all the way through to a station owned by another company). As well as the underground railway companies, these arrangements encompassed some of the main line railways, and the London United Tramways.

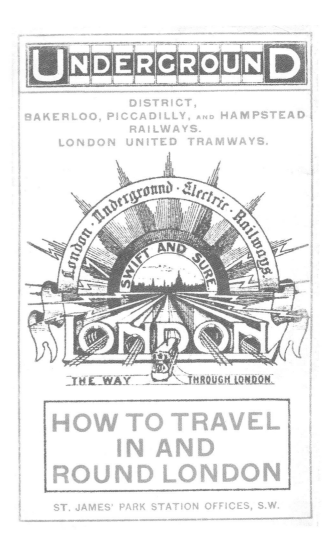

letters). Large illuminated signs were to be positioned on all stations, and a set of photographs of the stations was taken to have the signs drawn on to see the effect. Ceramic signs featuring the word, in white lettering on a mid-blue background, were added to many of the Leslie Green station buildings. The word TUBE was dropped.

The station platform name signs also received much attention. Photos from the early twentieth century show a confusion of advertising signs and posters, of all sizes, scattered over platform walls making it very hard for anyone to pick out the station name. Stanley, and his publicity manager Frank Pick recognized the problem and Pick ran experiments on the platform at St James's Park station, beneath the UERL's headquarters. Initially he placed the name in white lettering on a blue background across large white boards, to provide room to distinguish the name from the advertisements. The visibility of these was then increased by pasting red semicircles above and below the bar – the roundel was born (although it was known as the 'bullseye' for the early decades of its existence). The new style of name sign was rapidly rolled out across the District, Bakerloo, Piccadilly, and Hampstead lines.

Branding was another area for co-ordination. In 1907, Sir George Gibb had appointed a new General Manager to the UERL, called Albert Stanley. His previous role had been managing the tramways in New Jersey – another example of American influence over the company, although Stanley had been born in England. At the end of 1907, Stanley persuaded the other companies to jointly promote their combined network using the word UndergrounD (with larger end

Passengers were encouraged to get one of the maps that were being issued free of charge, under the distinctive UNDERGROUND branding. This leaflet was targeted at female passengers, possibly as part of the drive to boost off-peak traffic by shoppers.

Today, only Caledonian Road and Covent Garden stations retain roundel signs with a solid disc, dating back to the earliest form of the famous Underground sign. This example was at what is today named St Paul's station. The ease with which the red disc enabled passengers to spot the name of the station was the key to the success of the design.

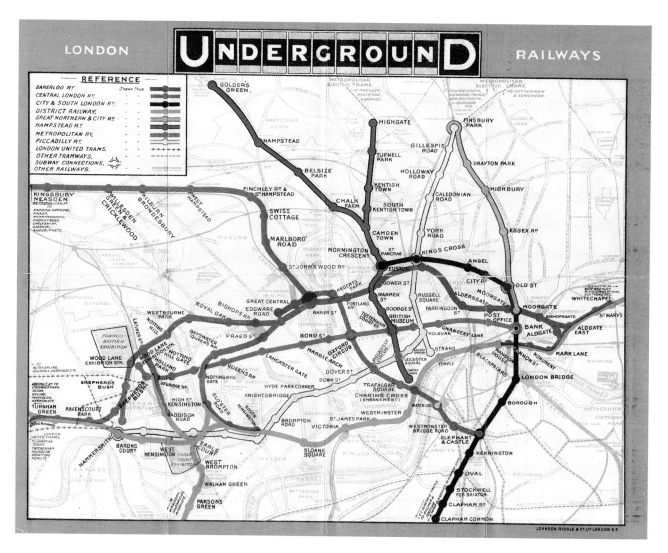

In 1907, the first official map of the underground railways (above) was issued: another result of the London Passenger Traffic Conference. No railway was given prominence over another, and each was shown in a different colour. The layout was broadly geographic, with a very faint map of major roads, main-line railways, parks, and the Thames as the background. Tramways connecting with the underground railways were shown in small dashed lines. The very first edition bore the title London Electric Railways above the map, but this was rapidly replaced by an edition featuring the UNDERGROUND logo.

The co-ordination of fares, interchanges and branding between the various underground companies in London in the years leading up to 1910 gave passengers a more unified impression. However, they had been financially traumatic for most of the companies. The UERL found that the financial innovations employed by Yerkes to raise the funding to build the lines were unsustainable, and after two years of debate and discussion between the various financiers involved, the company was restructured in 1908 following voluntary liquidation. In 1910, the Piccadilly legally took control of the Bakerloo and Hampstead Tubes under the name London Electric Railway (LER).

This poster was issued in 1912 to promote the benefits of season tickets to regular passengers. Of course, the company also benefited, through reduced ticket office costs (due to fewer transactions) and getting more money up front from passengers. The poster was designed by Tony Sarg.

The C&SLR was not in great financial shape either. Being the pioneer meant that it had non-standard equipment, most notably the small tunnels and trains, and was not in a position to raise the funds to do anything about the situation. The CLR had seen fierce competition along the parallel bus routes, which had caused drop in traffic. Experiments were made with cheaper fares for shorter distances, as well as off-peak tickets for shoppers, in order to build new business. A parcels service was introduced in 1911, with delivery boys on tricycles collecting and delivering from each station.

The worst performer of all of the tube railways was the GN&CR though. Its short length, location, and poor communication with the GNR at Finsbury Park had kept traffic levels down initially, and tramway competition from 1907 cut further into the numbers.

Moves toward unification occurred in 1912 and 1913. During 1912, both the Metropolitan Railway and the LER were making plans which resulted in the former purchasing the GN&CR, and the latter purchasing the CLR and C&SLR. The LER purchase took effect from 1 January 1913, and was made with the clear intention to modernize and enlarge the C&SLR. Later that same year, the MR assumed operation of the GN&CR, with the intention (thwarted in Parliament) of building a connection at Moorgate curving eastwards to join their existing railway at Liverpool Street. Hopes of another extension southwards, to connect with the Waterloo & City Railway at Bank were also dashed by opposition to the plans, and so the MR had to accept that they had bought a company with limited prospects.

The LER had, by comparison, bought two companies that had rather better potential. However, the C&SLR was going to require a large amount of investment in order to bring it up to standard. The extensive plans included work to enlarge the running tunnels to match the LER (11 ft 8¼ ins internal diameter), as well as extending it from Euston to join the Hampstead Tube at Camden Town.

The First Extensions

The C&SLR opened the first tube railway extension, in 1900. Its terminus at King William Street had always been awkward to operate, and the steep gradient on the approach had sometimes resulted in heavily-laden trains having to take a run up, or even have multiple attempts to reach the station. It had been reconstructed in 1895 to have two tracks with a single platform between, but this had not alleviated most of the problems. The company directors realized that the only solution was to build a new station in the City; the silver lining to the plan was that it would allow the railway to continue further north.

Work on the extension started in 1896, with the tunnels diverging just north of Borough station and forming a new crossing beneath the Thames. The opportunity was taken to provide a station at London Bridge, affording interchange with the main-line station. In the City of London, the replacement for King William Street was built in the crypt of the church of St Mary Woolnoth. The poor construction of the church caused many problems for the contractors, and cost the railway a significant sum in compensation. The line was continued further north to a temporary terminus at Moorgate Street, which allowed for interchange with the Metropolitan Railway. The new tunnels were built to the same size as the W&CR, the company having accepted the error of its original small tunnel diameter.

Also in 1900, the C&SLR opened a southward extension from its Stockwell terminus to Clapham Common (photo below). There was one intermediate station at Clapham Road (now Clapham North), and both of the new stations were built with narrow island platforms in large 30-ft diameter tunnels, which remain in use today and were at the time the largest bored tunnels in the world.

The following year, a three-station extension was opened from Moorgate Street to the Angel, via stations at Old Street and City Road. Angel had a layout similar to Clapham North and Common, which due to increased station usage was rebuilt with a separate northbound platform in 1992 on safety grounds.

This view shows the original 1900 station at Clapham Common. The use of brick and cream stone makes the building similar to the stations opened in 1890, but the main difference is the lack of a dome. The tendency of the day to cover surfaces in advertising for the company is very clearly shown. The two detail views opposite show the notices each side of the entrance.

The C&SLR was extended as far as Euston in 1907, and the station building (above) was provided on Eversholt Street. The left-hand photograph is of the western end of the platform. The terminus was a single tube, 30 feet in diameter, with tracks either side of an island platform. The staircase at the end of the platform led up to a long sloping passageway to the Hampstead Tube platforms. Lifts at the top of the stairs ascended into the main line station.

The Underground was rightly proud of its engineering works, and over the years a number of posters have shown cutaway diagrams of stations. This was one of the first, showing the straightforward connection that the escalators provided into Paddington main-line station from the new extension of the Bakerloo line in 1913. It is not completely accurate, since the running tunnels are parallel to the escalators in reality, whilst the poster makes it look like they only connect to one of the two platforms.

The only one of the Yerkes tubes to be extended before the First World War was the Bakerloo. It was first prolonged a short distance southwards, to a terminus at Elephant & Castle in August 1906. Low-level passageways allowed interchange with the C&SLR platforms there. At the other end of the line, although Baker Street was the terminus as far as passengers were concerned, trains continued to run as far as the unopened platforms beneath the main-line station at Marylebone. These were finally opened in March 1907, by which time construction of a further extension to Edgware Road was well under way.

West of Edgware Road, a long debate stalled further progress. Paddington had been the preferred terminus since an extension there had been promoted unsuccessfully in 1899. This would have had the station tunnels beneath the canal basin, with a single tunnel beyond leading to a depot on the surface north of Little Venice. Opposition from the Metropolitan Railway caused this plan to be rejected, but in 1900 the BS&WR successfully promoted a Bill that would have placed their Paddington station at Bishop's Road. A long tunnel beneath Eastbourne Terrace would have provided the connection into the main-line station. The positioning of the station would permit the company to further extend the line to either Royal Oak or Willesden, although these were just aspirations.

The poor interchange via the subway caused the company to have a rethink, and in 1906 a new Bill was approved. This changed the route so that the tunnels would follow along what is now the line of the Westway before curving southwards to tube platforms alongside the main-line station concourse. A pair of sidings would lie beyond, with the tunnels finishing at Sussex Gardens. This plan provided far better interchange with the Great Western Railway, and avoided the problems caused by the proximity of the canal, but left the railway pointing south-east – back towards central London rather than further toward the suburbs.

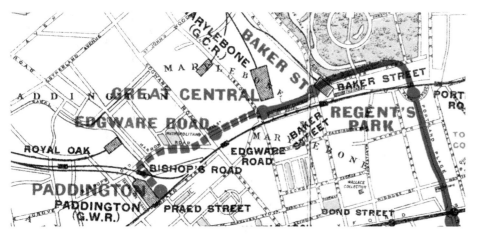

The original plan for the line at Paddington, forming a 'hook' that would face south-east can be seen; this awkward arrangement would have prevented any useful extension of the line, and caused a delay to this extension whilst a solution was sought. The station at Edgware Road was opened in June 1907.

In 1911 another route was put forward. This time the line would curve south-west from Edgware Road, and then swing sharply round to put the platforms alongside the western edge of the station, beneath the access ramp. In recognition of the improved connectivity that the tube railway would provide, the GWR contributed £18,000 to the costs of the extension, which now gave the Bakerloo an obvious route towards the suburbs. Construction work started in late 1911, and when it opened in 1913 the Bakerloo line station at Paddington was the first on the Underground to have escalators and no lifts. The previous year another BS&WR Bill had been deposited with Parliament for an extension of the line to Queen's Park station on the London & North Western Railway. The Bakerloo would rise to the surface and run its trains over the LNWR tracks as far as Watford Junction, which was achieved in 1917.

Consideration was also given to southern extensions of the Bakerloo, with the obvious route taking it to Camberwell. In 1913 the Lord Mayor of London suggested that the company was prepared to extend as far as Crystal Palace, via Camberwell and Dulwich. With the company's attention focused on the extension north-west, and the onset of the First World War, these ideas vanished into obscurity, Camberwell resurfacing from time to time until quite recently.

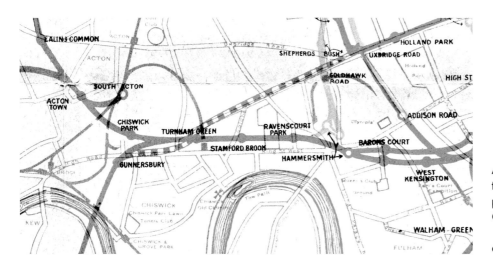

An extract from one of the few maps to show the proposed CLR extension to Gunnersbury, published in 1914. The direct course of the extension is made very clear.

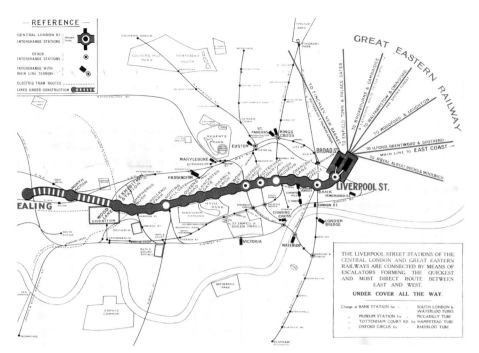

The Central London Railway produced a number of maps that strongly emphasized their own route through London, and this 1912 example is no exception. The other underground railways are thin black lines, less prominent even than the seven main-line routes shown radiating from Liverpool Street and Broad Street stations. The map was produced to advertise the opening of the extension of the CLR to the latter stations.

The first extension of the Central London Railway made use of the existing single line that ran west from Shepherd's Bush to the railway's depot at Wood Lane. The Anglo-French Exhibition of 1908 was to be held on land just across the road from the depot, and so by building another section of tunnel to link the depot site with the eastbound platform at Shepherd's Bush a complete loop was formed. A new station was made alongside Wood Lane, with a platform on either side of the single track to allow it to handle the expected crowds. It opened in 1908, on the same day as the exhibition.

At the other end of the line, the CLR had originally intended to run as far east as Liverpool Street. Difficulties in coming to an agreement with the Great Eastern Railway, which owned the main-line station, meant that this had been abandoned. Sidings to the east of Bank were built in the hope that they could act as the start of a future extension, and in 1910 work began on the construction of new tunnels and platforms beneath the main-line station. The new station was provided with escalators to both main-line stations at Broad Street and Liverpool Street, as well as lifts to Broad Street – this made it the first on the network to have escalators from its opening day, which was 28 July 1912.

With the extension to Liverpool Street approved, in 1911 the CLR successfully promoted a Bill for a short extension from the loop line at Wood Lane to the Ealing & Shepherd's Bush Railway (E&SBR), a new line being built by the GWR. This would allow CLR trains to reach Ealing. The First World War delayed completion of the E&SBR, and it was not until 1920 that the first passenger trains ran.

In 1913, the CLR sought powers to build another extension west, this time forming a branch from the line at Shepherd's Bush station. Tunnels would follow the direct course of the Goldhawk and Stamford Brook Roads as far as Turnham Green (with five new stations,

Circular tickets are highly unusual, and this example dates from 1912. It allows travel throughout the length of the line, but only after 10am, and only to ladies. Despite this, the lady is not permitted to have her own name on the ticket, but that of her husband or father (of whom she is the "lady representative"). The ticket is valid for the whole of December.

This view of parcels being transferred between a train and the platform at Post Office (now St Paul's) station illustrates the scale of the operation. The passenger numbers, and need to despatch trains quickly from platforms would make this service impossible to operate today. The service continued until 30 June 1917.

Signal Box with
8 TRACKS under
HUNGERFORD FOOTBRIDGE at side of CHARING CROSS RAILWAY BRIDGE
CHARING CROSS TERMINUS
SOUTH-EASTERN AND CHATHAM RAILWAY
ENTRANCE
EXIT
7-Car Train
DISTRICT RAILWAY
LCC TRAMWAYS
Showing TRAILER Cars used at "RUSH" HOURS
West-bound Platform
Emergency Pump installed during War to prevent flooding of tube beneath River through possible air raid damage
North-bound PLATFORM
5-Car Train
Escalator Up
Subway
Escalator down
South-bound PLATFORM
BAKERLOO Railway passes beneath RIVER here
6-Car Train
Train approaching from Strand Stn.
HAMPSTEAD Railway Terminal Loop
FROM THE "GRAPHIC."

including Turnham Green), beyond which it would curve west then south to join the London & South Western Railway just north of Gunnersbury station. The intention was that the CLR trains would run through to Shepperton via Richmond.

World War I delayed the start of construction, and aside from Bills to extend the time permitted to build the new line, nothing further was done. After the war a new route via Hammersmith was considered, but instead the Underground group decided to extend the Piccadilly line west from Hammersmith to Acton.

The final tube extension of the pre-war period was opened in 1914. It was on the Hampstead Tube, and prolonged it a short distance south to a single-platform station at Charing Cross (Embankment). This gave interchange with both the District and Bakerloo lines, thus providing a direct interchange which previously had involved passengers walking between the Strand and the station at Embankment at street level. The extension was built in the form of a loop extending out beneath the Thames, allowing trains to reverse without the driver having to change ends and enabling the extension to be served by a single platform, albeit on a rather sharp curve.

Above An isometric drawing of Charing Cross (Embankment) station following the opening of the loop on the Hampstead Tube and the introduction of escalators. The sharply curved loop platform can be seen.

Facing page This postcard from 1909 sought to boost off-peak traffic from shoppers.

Safety

Although the tube railways had over half a century of railway experience on which to base their operating practices, the uniquely different environment in which they ran meant that to a large extent they were developing their ways of working from scratch. It is not surprising to find that despite the almost military discipline that the companies sought to exert over their staff, situations arose for which no one was prepared, and improvisation was called for. An example of this was on the steep gradient approaching the City terminus at King William Street station on the C&SLR, where it was not unknown for trains to stall if heavily laden. When this happened, the locomotive crew would let the train roll backwards to the foot of the gradient and take a run-up for a second go. If this failed, a spare locomotive from King William Street would be run back towards the train and couple on to the front in order to provide extra power. That this did not result in accidents was due to the signalling system, which did not permit a train to leave Borough station until the previous train had arrived at the City.

Passengers were not officially permitted to ride on the platforms at the ends of the carriages, and the wisdom of this rule was demonstrated when one slipped – possibly he was crossing between the locomotive and the first carriage, having been invited to do so by a member of staff – and fell to his death beneath the train.

The lifts, with their manually operated gates, were another source of danger. There was originally no interlocking to ensure that the gates were closed before the lift could move and in the first year of operation a passenger running for a lift that had started before the gates were shut caught his foot in the mechanism and was pulled upwards by the lift and decapitated.

One of the major fears on the tube railways was fire. The confined spaces, strong draughts created by the trains acting like pistons through the tunnels, and new technology of electricity combined to provide a high risk. One of the first significant fires took place in January 1902, on a locomotive between Elephant & Castle and Borough stations. A short-circuit in the controller (the device used by the driver to regulate the speed) caused the insulation and then the teak cabinet housing the controller to ignite. The following train pushed the train into Borough, but the flames were fanned by the draught and the carriage behind the locomotive was also damaged as a result. Fortunately no passengers or staff were injured.

The substation at Notting Hill Gate station on the CLR suffered a serious fire in April 1905. Access was made more difficult because the substation was located at the bottom of one of the lift shafts, below the lower lift landing. After a transformer caught fire, the air blowing through the tunnels fanned the flames, igniting cable insulation.

The CLR left the space beneath the sleepers open, fearing that the use of ballast would lead to dust building up in the tunnels. To allow maintenance staff access, and for passenger evacuation in the event of a broken-down train, boards were laid between the central conductor rail and one of the running rails. The thought that a passenger walking in a dimly lit tunnel might step over the central rail and fall through the sleepers seems either to have not occurred, or been dismissed. The 1904 fire regulations required that future tube railways filled this space. Although not retrospective, the existing companies gradually complied over the following years. This pre-opening drawing of Holland Park station comes from a contemporary German journal and also shows the wooden platform, which was replaced by non-flammable materials within a decade.

The substation attendants tripped the circuit breakers and hastily left. When the fire brigade arrived they dismissed the warnings of the Substation Superintendent to check that the power was off, telling him "When we are called in, we take charge." A loud roar from within the substation made the brigade officer reconsider, and he waited until the current had been cut off at the power station before his men tackled the fire. This led to substantial changes to the CLR substations to prevent a reoccurrence.

Fire regulations were introduced by the Board of Trade in 1904, as a result of a major fire on the Paris Métro the previous year. These regulations specified that trains had to be made of steel as far as possible, with any wood used treated to make it inflammable, 25% of the lighting underground to be powered from a separate supply, all exits to be lit conspicuously, and that woodwork should be eliminated from areas below ground. The CLR platforms, for example, were all made of wood which was soon replaced by stone slabs.

The regulations were not retrospective however, and so the CLR platform changes were made voluntarily. The C&SLR was slower in removing its woodwork, which led to a major fire in the evening of 16 July 1908. It appears to have started on the track just south of Moorgate station – the company using pitch pine for its sleepers, which was flammable. Although station staff tried to extinguish it, trains continued to run, which probably fanned the flames. About ten minutes after it was first noticed, the smoke was getting thicker, and the station was evacuated. The fire brigade was called 20 minutes later, but were unable to get to the tunnel because of the smoke. They tried to access it via the next station to the north, Old Street, but again the smoke was too thick. They finally managed to reach it from Bank station, pumping water through hoses along the tunnel. The fire was found to have spread to the wood structure of a disused signal cabin, in the roof of a large crossover tunnel. Dirt and rubbish that had filled the space in the tunnel beneath the sleepers was also to blame, and the company filled this space in subsequently.

The First Escalators

With a handful of exceptions, all of the underground stations on the first tube lines had access to their platforms via lifts. (The exceptions were both the stations on the W&CR, and Gillespie Road on the Piccadilly Tube). It was the invention of the lift, together with the critical safety braking equipment, in the late 1800s that made railways such as London's tubes possible, as passengers could not have been expected to walk up and down flights of stairs to the necessary depths. However, lifts had their disadvantages as well. They are an intermittent mode of transport: passengers are transported in batches, and most passengers will either have to wait for a lift car to arrive at the level where they are, or will have to wait in the lift car until it is ready to depart. As the tube railways became busier. Something better was needed.

The better machine was the escalator, familiar to everyone who uses the Underground today. In the first years of the twentieth century though, it was a novelty, and not quite ready for intensive use. Various machines were installed in the USA in the 1890s which have been described as escalators, although since they did not form steps they should really be called moving walkways. Similar machines were installed in Harrod's store in Knightsbridge in 1898, the Crystal Palace in 1900, and at Seaforth Sands station on the Liverpool Overhead Railway in 1901. A highly unusual, experimental spiral conveyor was installed in a shaft at Holloway Road station on the Piccadilly Tube in 1906, but would not appear to have entered passenger service. It was another five years before the tubes acquired their first escalator.

Two escalators have been installed at Earl's Court station by the District Railway for the rapid transference of passengers between its own line and that of the Brompton and Piccadilly Railway. The escalator underwent a Board of Trade inspect-ion on Tuesday, and on Wednesday was opened for the use of the public. Four escalators will also be installed in the extension of the Central London Railway to Liverpool Street Station.

In the opinion of the traffic manager of the Central London Railway these moving staircases are far better than lifts for tube railway work, and no new tube station will be constructed without them. The escalator has the appearance of an ordinary stairway, four feet wide, which moves noiselessly onward and upward until, when near the top, the step on which the passenger stands falls off it its rate of rise, allowing the step in the rear to gain on it, when the upward movement ceases and the steps move forward horizontally in the form of a platform, from which, with the aid of a travelling hand-rail, even the most nervous of passengers can step without fear of shock or accident. Should the machinery by any chance fail the escalator can still be used as an ordinary stairway.

A NEW STAIR LIFT.

THE NEW AUTOMATIC STAIRCASE, NOW WORKING AT EARL'S COURT STATION, WHICH CONVEYS PASSENGERS FROM THE PICCADILLY TUBE TO THE LEVEL OF THE DISTRICT RAILWAY.

The station chosen was Earl's Court, with a pair of escalators installed in a single inclined shaft that linked the platform level of the Piccadilly with a new concourse beneath the District Railway platforms. It is possible that Earl's Court was chosen because the lifts from the Piccadilly platforms took passengers to ticket hall level, some distance above the District platforms, and so this would make a more convenient interchange. There was also space at the lower level between the platforms, making the connection even easier. The manufacturer was the Otis Elevator Company, who had provided all of the lifts at the UERL stations.

Below The early escalators had distinctive 'shunt' endings that forced passengers to step off sideways, as shown in this photograph of one of the new machines at Charing Cross in 1914. The steps were also flat, with the cleated designs introduced in the 1920s.

Right Despite the first escalators having opened over two years previously, they were still enough of a novelty to be featured prominently on this handbill issued by the Underground company to advertise their services to football fans attending the match between Liverpool and Aston Villa football fans in 1914.

Opposite A page from the *Illustrated London News* of the day.

The design of the escalator was rather different from those installed today. The steps had flat wooden tops, without grooves, and at the 'departure' end was a shunt. This was a diagonally positioned wall across the steps that forced passengers to step sideways (left at Earl's Court) to get off. The shunts were intended to prevent feet getting trapped at the end as the stairs looped back under the escalator. The down escalator had a shunt at both ends, as it was possible to reverse it in the event of the up escalator being out of service. This meant that both escalators had shunts at the upper landing, forcing the descending machine to have a very long level section between the shunt and the shaft. A leather belt ran across the lower edge of the end shunts between two vertical rollers, so that anyone remaining on the escalator and coming into contact with the shunt would be pushed sideways and off the machine.

Passengers found the escalators a novelty, with some travelling to Earl's Court just to ride on the new machines. Around 550,000 used them in the first month; during this time, dress guards were added to reduce the incidents of ladies clothing becoming trapped and torn. The machine required its own inspection by the Board of Trade (which authorized railway works for public use), and a second inspection was insisted upon after a month in service. This found that the machines were 'reasonably safe', and gave full permission for their use thereafter.

ASTON VILLA
v.
LIVERPOOL

SATURDAY, MARCH 28th, 1914
KICK-OFF AT 3.30 p.m.

At

Tottenham Hotspurs Football Ground

THE BEST WAY
to reach the Match

From PADDINGTON is by

(BAKERLOO LINE).

THE LARGEST MOVING STAIRWAYS IN THE WORLD

Connect the Great Western Station with the Bakerloo Railway.

Book Through to
FINSBURY PARK
From Paddington.

TRAMS & MOTOR-BUSES RUN FROM THERE
DIRECT TO THE GROUND.

The following year, more escalators appeared on the network. The CLR opened its extension to Liverpool Street, and this included a pair of escalators between the platforms and the new ticket hall, as well as a second pair that took passengers into Broad Street station. These were of the same type that had been installed at Earl's Court, but here they were each fitted into their own single shafts.

AN ENDLESS CHAIN OF STAIRS: THE ESCALATOR.

DRAWINGS BY W. B. ROBINSON; PHOTOGRAPH BY CHARLES J. CLARKE.

THE ESCALATOR EMPLOYED FOR CONVEYING MATERIALS

THE TRAVELLING RUBBER HANDRAIL PASSING OVER THE TOP WHEEL (Panel removed)

THE EARL'S COURT ESCALATOR (SECTIONAL VIEW)

District Railway Platform Earl's Court Station

Upper Chamber

THE NEW ESCALATOR at EARL'S COURT SHOWING SECTION WITH MACHINERY CHAMBER

Machinery Chamber

VIEW WITH SEVERAL STEPS REMOVED SHOWING THE RUNNING GEAR OF THE ESCALATOR.

THE LOWER CHAMBER AND TUBE RAILWAY PLATFORM EARL'S COURT ESCALATOR

The Last Year of Peace

The many bold plans for London's tube railways, mostly made in the aftermath of the company acquisitions of 1913, were dashed by the outbreak of war in summer 1914. The focus for the next four years would be on keeping the railways running under very different circumstances than the previous decade had brought.

The plans for the C&SLR to be enlarged and joined with the Hampstead Tube have been mentioned in a previous chapter. In 1914, there were also authorized plans to extend one of the Hampstead Tube's northern branches from Golders Green to Edgware. At Hammersmith, a westward extension of the Piccadilly Tube onto the disused tracks of the London & South Western Railway. These tracks would allow Piccadilly trains to run parallel to those of the District Railway as far as Richmond. Also in west London, the CLR had an authorized extension from Shepherd's Bush to Gunnersbury via Goldhawk Road, and on to Richmond (which, it appeared, would be served by a plethora of railway companies). All of these works, with the exception of the CLR extension, would be completed by the early 1930s.

An extension of the CLR which did come to fruition was that to Ealing Broadway. This made use of the Ealing & Shepherd's Bush Railway (E&SBR), promoted by the Great Western Railway, and which was completed during the war. By means of a short connecting line leading north from their terminus loop at White City, the CLR would join the E&SBR and operate its services through to Ealing, although these did not start running until 1920.

SEASON TICKETS
! ! !

DO YOU KNOW YOU CAN NOW HAVE A

SEASON TICKET

ON THE

Central London Tube Railway

BETWEEN ANY STATIONS ?

BEST VALUE IN LONDON

Monthly, Quarterly, Annually

OZONAIR FREE

Apply for Particulars at Manager's Office, Oxford Circus Station, w.

The Bakerloo Tube was in the process of being extended north-west from Paddington to join the LNWR at Queen's Park. The outbreak of war slowed the works due to the shortage of labour, but they were sufficiently advanced to allow the extension to open in 1915, via intermediate stations at Warwick Avenue, Maida Vale, and Kilburn Park. All three were built with escalators to the platforms, and in a style clearly derived from that of Leslie Green. The extension achieved another 'first' for the Underground when Maida Vale station opened in June 1915 staffed entirely by women.

Another CLR innovation being installed in 1914, was a novel ventilation system called Ozonair. From its opening days the line had been plagued by criticism of a musty smell, although several scientific investigations had found nothing wrong with the air in the tunnels. Nevertheless, in 1911 a decision was made to install equipment in the station ventilation which added ozone to the air that was pumped down to the platforms. This was described at the time as giving the air "a most agreeable and refreshing odour, similar to that met with at the seaside or mountain top".

NEW LONDON "TUBE" STATION WHICH IS STAFFED ENTIRELY BY WOMEN.

Porter carrying bags.

"All tickets," says the collector at the lift door.

The booking clerk issuing tickets.

They all wear uniform.

Ten young women between the ages of eighteen and twenty-five comprise the staff of the new Bakerloo "Tube" Station at Maida Vale, which was opened yesterday. They perform exactly the same duties as men, and are paid at exactly the same rates as male employees performing similar duties.—(*Daily Mirror* and L.N.A.)

ON THE BAKERLOO TUBE: A GATE-OPERATOR
AT WORK.

Women are now employed on the Bakerloo Tube Railway, and one is seen in our photograph, at work on the train. They have already shown aptitude and commendable care in the discharge of their duties.—[*Photograph by L.N.A.*]

Left Women also took on roles on the trains (except that of driver). A female gate operator on the Bakerloo line is shown in this cutting from a contemporary magazine.

Right Wartime austerity is probably the reason for this poster being limited to black and white text. It was issued to mark the opening of the first stage of the Bakerloo line extension beyond Paddington on 31 January 1915. Trains served the two stations mentioned, Maida Vale not being ready, and then ran empty to Queen's Park which was also not quite complete and opened ten days later.

The start of the First World War disrupted the Underground just as it started to consolidate operations across the various lines. There were two major companies now involved: the Underground group, controlling the Bakerloo, Piccadilly, and Hampstead Tubes, the District Railway, the CLR, and the C&SLR, together with most of the major tramways and bus operators; and the Metropolitan Railway, which owned the GN&CR. All of these companies had big plans for extension and improvement which suddenly had to be put on hold as the country faced new challenges, and it would be the 1920s before significant progress would be made in improving London's transport.

THE WAR-TIME VALUE OF WORDS.

"HURRY UP THERE, PLEASE! PLENTY OF ROOM DOWN THE CENTRE OF THE CAR."

Above There was no suitable site for a street level building at Warwick Avenue so part of the road was built on for a stairway down to the booking hall. Maida Vale and Kilburn Park had buildings with similar red terracotta styling as used by Leslie Green.

Left Although the age of the platform staff and methods for getting passengers onto trains have been exaggerated in this cartoon from Punch, the First World War saw a noticeable increase in passenger numbers on the Underground due to troop movements and reduced bus services due to the vehicles being sent to the trenches. The cartoon shows the difficulties encountered with carriages that could only be boarded from the ends — passengers were reluctant to move down inside lest they be unable to get out when needed.

Bibliography

Newspapers and periodicals

Black and White Budget magazine
The Bystander
The Daily Graphic
The Daily Mail
The Daily Mirror
The Daily Telegraph
The Engineer
Engineering
The Evening News
The Globe
The Graphic
Hackney & Kingsland Gazette
The Illustrated London News
The London Magazine
The London Standard
The Londoner
The Penny Illustrated Paper
Punch
The Railway Magazine
The Railway Times
The South London Press
The Times
Tramway & Railway World
Underground News

Books

Badsey-Ellis, Antony, *London's Lost Tube Schemes* (Capital Transport 2005)
Badsey-Ellis, Antony, *Underground Heritage* (Capital Transport 2012)
Badsey-Ellis, Antony, *Building London's Underground* (Capital Transport 2016)
Bownes, David, Green, Oliver and Mullins, Sam, *Underground – How the Tube Shaped London* (Allen Lane, 2012)
Croome, Desmond and Jackson, Alan, *Rails Through the Clay* (Capital Transport 1993)
Day, John, and Reed, John, *The Story of London's Underground*, 12th edition (Capital Transport 2019)
Gillham, John, *The Waterloo & City Railway* (Oakwood Press 2001)
Holman, Printz P., *The Amazing Electric Tube* (London Transport Museum 1990)
Leboff, David, *The Underground Stations of Leslie Green* (Capital Transport 2002)
Rose, Douglas, *Tiles of the Unexpected Underground* (Douglas Rose 2007)
Taylor, Sheila (Ed.), *The Moving Metropolis* (Lawrence King 2001)
Wilson, B. and Stewart Haram, V., *The Central London Railway* (Fairseat Press 1950)